THE EVERYDAY SUPERFOOD

Kale

THE EVERYDAY SUPERFOOD

Kale

150 Nutritious Recipes
to Delight Every Kind of Eater

FALL RIVER PRESS

New York

FALL RIVER PRESS

New York

An Imprint of Sterling Publishing
1166 Avenue of the Americas
New York, NY 10036

Cover design by Elizabeth Lindy

ISBN 978-1-4351-6235-8

For information about custom editions, special sales, and premium and corporate purchases,
please contact Sterling Special Sales at 800-805-5489 or specialsales@sterlingpublishing.com.

Manufactured in China

2 4 6 8 10 9 7 5 3 1

www.sterlingpublishing.com

Kale for Every Day

Five Unexpected Ways to Incorporate Kale into Your Meals

Try savory oatmeal instead of sweet. Oatmeal is just as good even when you exclude the brown sugar and cinnamon in favor of sautéed kale and a poached egg. Cook regular or steel-cut oats according to package instructions, add them to a skillet full of kale, and top with a perfectly poached egg.

Keep frozen kale pesto on hand to pop into sauces, smoothies, and main courses. Make kale pesto with garlic, cashews, and extra-virgin olive oil; then spoon the finished product into ice cube trays for whenever your recipes need a tasty and healthy lift.

Quench your thirst with kale lemonade. Juice an entire bunch of kale, stir it into a pitcher of water and lemon juice, and add a touch of sugar, fresh ginger and mint, and heaps of ice cubes.

Satisfy your sweet tooth. Puréed kale or powdered kale can be mixed into a decadent brownie batter, and no one will suspect a thing. The earthy taste brings out the chocolate, and the puréed greens add a fabulous moistness.

Grill it up. Hamburgers of any kind, from vegan to hearty beef creations, benefit from the addition of finely chopped kale. The greens add nutrients, flavor, and moistness to the finished burger.

Contents

8 Hand-Helds 189

9 Main Dishes 209

Introduction

Not only is kale delicious (but you already know that), it's prized for being one of the most powerful, nutrient-rich vegetables. In fact, before cabbage came along, kale dominated dishes in Europe for hundreds of years.

While kale has become a trendy term that's tossed around in culinary circles and foodie blogs, this superfood has actually been enjoyed by our ancestors for centuries. Is it really any surprise? At approximately 30 calories per serving, this nutrient-dense powerhouse is one of the healthiest veggies you can put on your plate—and in your mouth.

No doubt you've already joined the kale craze. And we don't blame you. That single low-calorie serving provides a whole day's worth of Vitamin C, double the daily intake of Vitamin A, and almost seven times your recommended daily dose of Vitamin K. And let's not forget kale's rich amount of flavonoids, plant compounds with powerful antioxidant and anti-inflammatory properties.

But maybe you're bored with your current kale dishes and looking for ways to go beyond the basics.

Kale: The Everyday Superfood invites you to celebrate this versatile veggie and discover endless ways to enjoy kale as a side-dish staple, steamed or sautéed in main courses, served in tasty salads, and even whipped into decadent desserts.

Featuring over 150 easy and tasty recipes, this book will help you discover why this user-friendly crop deserves its superfood status.

Kale: The Everyday Superfood will prepare you to reap the benefits of this veggie, with useful information on how to:

- Establish better eating habits by incorporating kale into your routine

- Preserve fresh, beautiful greens with storage and prep tips

- Prepare time-saving "one-pot" recipes that take the chaos out of cooking

- Distinguish the most popular types of kale that are best for eating

Don't let its sturdy leaves fool you. Though its tougher texture can make kale more challenging to cook compared with other greens, the recipes offered here are creative, accessible, and delicious. The few extra minutes of cooking time will be well worth it.

With kale there's truly something for everyone—right down to the youngest and pickiest eaters in your household. Introducing your kids to veggies, and kale, as part of a regular diet *is* possible. And we'll show you how. Our tasty superfood ideas will bring everyone in your family to the table and guarantee kale's status as kid-approved.

Entice your kids with family-friendly and nutritious dishes, including:

- Colorful Breakfast Wraps

- Kale-Chicken Pizza

- Kale & Turkey Roll-Ups

Helpful labels throughout this book will guide you toward diet-specific dishes. So whether you're a meat lover, strict vegan, prefer Paleo, or go gluten-free, you can refer to the handy, clearly labeled recipes to meet your specific dietary needs.

In *Kale: The Everyday Superfood,* you will learn why kale is king. Its stellar nutritional profile has been backed by numerous studies, which indicate that kale can:

- Protect against cancer.

- Help lower blood sugar.

- Reduce the risk of heart disease.

- Support healthy bones and teeth.

- Promote healthy glowing skin and thick hair.

Kale: The Everyday Superfood will get you started in enjoying the nutritious benefits and tasty surprises of kale. Passing fad? Hardly. This book proves that kale is definitely here to stay.

1

The Best of the Bunch(es)

Now that you have committed to kale in all its tasty variations, you might want more information on this superfood. Kale is a lovely leafy green (red, white, or bluish) cruciferous vegetable. It's been used for years as a frilly garnish on buffets or restaurant plates, but why is it suddenly so desirable and valued?

The rise of kale's status in North America is relatively recent, but kale has been on the culinary radar in many countries for centuries because it is spectacularly nutritious, versatile, and delicious. It also doesn't hurt, as noted previously, that kale is incredibly easy to grow—even when the frost comes—and can provide a constant supply of tender leaves for months when other plants have withered away. Kale is here to stay, so let's take a closer look at kale in all its delicious, healthy glory.

Why Is Kale a Superfood?

Superfood seems to be a term loosely tossed around these days, so it's easy to be skeptical about the pedigree of foods labeled as such. Never fear: Kale is one of the most nutritious foods in the world, and the health benefits of this delicious vegetable are unassailable. You don't have to consume bushels of kale to reap the rewards. Kale is so rich in nutrients that as little as one to two cups per day can have a significant positive impact on your health. If you're asking why kale is such a superfood, consider all that it can do for you as you massage kale leaves or bake kale chips in the oven:

Absorb free radicals. Kale is one of the most highly ranked foods on the Oxygen Radical Absorbance Capacity (ORAC) rating scale because of its high antioxidant content. ORAC measures the capacity of foods to scavenge free radicals in the body. Free radicals damage the body's cells, causing diseases like cardiovascular disease, several autoimmune diseases, type 2 diabetes, atherosclerosis, and macular degeneration of the eye. As noted by researchers Christine B. Ambrosone and Li Tang in a 2009 article in *Cancer Research Prevention*, removing free radicals from the body, or neutralizing them, can cut your risk of disease considerably.

Protect against cancer. You may not have heard of glucosinolates, but these sulfur-containing chemicals are responsible for the bitter taste and unique smell of cruciferous vegetables. The specific glucosinolates in kale include glucobrassicin, glucoraphanin, and sinigrin, which break down into compounds called indoles and isothiocyanates when kale is chewed and digested. In their 2008 book, *Cancer Letters,* John D. Clarke and his co-authors note that these compounds can help prevent several cancers, such as bladder, breast, colon, liver, lung, ovarian, prostate, and stomach cancers. Indoles and isothiocyanates have been shown to:

- » Inactivate carcinogens
- » Induce cancer cell death
- » Inhibit tumor blood vessel formation needed for metastasis
- » Protect cells from DNA damage
- » Suppress the growth of cancer tumors

Support urinary tract health. According to a study in a 2008 issue of *Cancer Epidemiology Biomarkers & Prevention*, kale not only helps prevent bladder cancer, it can also contribute to enhanced overall urinary tract health, including fighting urinary tract infections (UTIs). Kale is packed with nutrients such as vitamin A that support urinary tract health. Healthy linings mean lower infection rates, which is why kale is one of the most highly recommended foods for preventing and treating UTIs.

Promote eye health. A recent article from WebMD, "The Truth About Kale," identifies kale as a stellar source of the antioxidants lutein and zeaxanthin as well as vitamin A, all of which are crucial for eye health. Kale has a combined 26 milligrams of lutein and zeaxanthin per serving to protect the eyes. Kale's vitamin A content is over 200 percent of the recommended daily amount. Vitamin A is also linked to a reduced risk of macular degeneration as well as helping extend vision in people with retinitis pigmentosa.

Help lower blood sugar. Kale is rich in fiber and an antioxidant called alpha-lipoic acid, making it a very effective choice for lowering blood sugar. One cup of kale contains almost three grams of fiber, about 10 to 15 percent of the recommended daily amount. A high-fiber diet can lower blood glucose levels and improve insulin levels. Alpha-lipoic acid can also lower blood sugar levels while increasing insulin sensitivity, making insulin more effective in the body.

Reduce the risk of heart disease. Kale is packed with heart-healthy components such as potassium, vitamin C, fiber, and omega-3 fatty acids. If you have heart disease or an increased risk for it, one of the most important recommendations from your doctor is to increase your potassium intake and reduce sodium in your diet. Kale is very high in potassium, which can increase the dilation of the blood vessels, lowering blood pressure. According to The Nutrition Source from Harvard's School of Public Health, adding kale to your diet goes a long way toward reaching the recommended goal of 4,700 milligrams of potassium per day, which can lower your risk of heart disease by 49 percent and decrease your risk of dying from any disease by 20 percent. The fiber in kale can protect you from atherosclerosis and lower cholesterol levels, while the omega-3 fatty acids decrease triglyceride levels, lower blood pressure, and reduce the risk of blood clots.

Support healthy bones and teeth. What should you consume for strong bones and teeth? You probably think "milk" immediately because of its calcium content. But wait—kale is a better source of calcium that the body can absorb more easily. In milk, calcium is attached to casein—a protein that is difficult for some people to digest. Because of this, the calcium in cow's milk is not utilized as well by the body. Why is this? To break down casein, the body needs to produce lots of hydrochloric acid, which creates an acidic environment that leaches calcium out of the bones. Kale is alkalizing in the body, meaning the amount of calcium needed to neutralize acid is less, creating less of a demand. Kale is also incredibly high in vitamin K, needed to improve calcium absorption and decrease the amount of calcium excreted in the urine. Vitamin K deficiency has been linked with an increased risk of bone fractures.

Promote healthy, glowing skin and healthy hair. The abundant antioxidants in kale can have an extremely positive effect on your skin and hair. The largest bodily organ, skin is constantly bombarded by ultraviolet radiation and free radicals. According to Joel Fuhrman, a board-certified family physician, *New York Times* best-selling author, and recognized expert on nutrition, the antioxidants in kale can fight the effects of this assault, helping prevent the loss of elasticity in the skin. You will see fewer fine lines and wrinkles when eating kale regularly. Your hair will also benefit because the iron plus vitamins A and C in kale are necessary for healthy hair. An iron deficiency can cause hair loss, so keeping that level up can help your locks stay thick. Vitamin A supports the sebum production required to moisturize hair and help it grow, while vitamin C builds the collagen needed to make hair strong with good structure.

Strengthen your immune system. Kale contains over 80 milligrams of immune-boosting vitamin C per serving. This vitamin repairs the body's tissues, promotes cell growth, helps heal wounds, and fights free-radical cell damage. Vitamin C is not stored in the body, so it is important to get enough through food sources like kale. Vitamin C levels are very sensitive to stress, and excessive stress can seriously compromise the immune system. Eating kale can ensure your immune system stays strong and works effectively for good health.

Getting the Whole Picture of Kale

THE LEAF LIST

Kale's many varieties display a range of color spanning from yellow all the way to almost black. This versatile vegetable is sometimes classified by the form and texture of its leaves, and not all varieties are suitable for culinary needs. Some of the most popular types include:

Blue Armor (45 to 75 days to maturity). A lovely, deep blue-green kale with fringed and very curled leaves, Blue Armor is a hardy, Scotch-type plant (characterized by ruffled, dark green, almost blue leaves) suitable for fall or spring plantings.

GROW YOUR OWN?

Buying organic kale can get pricey if you plan to include this spectacular green in your meals regularly. Growing your own kale is a viable option to offset some grocery costs, and it is relatively easy to get a good crop. A cool weather crop, kale does not like heat. It can be started indoors about four to six weeks before your typical last frost date in the spring and can stand temperatures as low as 20°F. The seedlings should be about six weeks old when transplanted to the garden, and you should time your harvest to occur before temperatures reach 80°F.

You can also start kale outdoors from seeds. Plant them half an inch deep about two to four weeks before your typical last frost date, spaced about three inches apart. When the plants reach about five inches in height, thin them so they are about one foot apart. Kale also grows well in containers as small as six inches wide.

Kale prefers well-fertilized, high-quality soil but can grow in most mixes. Kale does well in sunlight, as long as it is not scorching hot. You should water your plants well because thirsty plants can produce tough leaves. If you have access to straw, kale benefits from straw mounded around the stems once the plants are about six inches high so the leaves don't touch the soil. Although kale does not have any serious disease issues, it can be the target of many pests such as cutworms, cabbageworms, flea beetles, and aphids.

Within 80 days after starting the kale seeds, the greens should be ready to harvest. When the plants are 10 inches high and the leaves are about the size of your hand, snip the outside leaves off to use in recipes. This careful cutting will allow the plant to continue to grow. You can also cut the entire plant about two inches above the soil. The cut section will grow new leaves in a couple of weeks.

You can continue to harvest the kale as long as the leaves keep growing in, sometimes all winter depending on your climate. If you find your kale plants covered in snow, don't despair. In about mid-February, the kale will start to grow again, and you can harvest the leaves well into June and sometimes even later. When you stop snipping leaves and the kale starts to put out buds, you can also eat those. The seedpods will eventually turn brown and dry out if you stop snipping them off. Just keep them dry, and you will have kale seeds to plant again for another delicious crop.

Blue Knight (55 days to maturity). Similar to Blue Armor, with a deep blue-green color and curly leaves, this is also a Scotch-type kale. It is slow to bolt (run to seed) and good for fall and spring plantings, or as a winter-long crop in the southern United States.

Blue Ridge (60 days to maturity). This kale, characterized by fully curled leaves in a dark blue-green color, is popular in all areas that produce kale commercially. The leaves are firm enough to be suitable for hand or mechanical stripping.

Dwarf Blue Curled (55 days to maturity). An attractive, low-growing kale with a pretty blue-green color and finely curled leaves, this variety is very hardy and holds its color in severe cold. You can harvest Dwarf Blue Curled Kale all winter in temperate regions because it is one of the most frost-resistant varieties. It is also known as Dwarf Blue Scotch, Dwarf Blue Curled Scotch, Blue Curled Scotch, and Dwarf Blue Curled Vates.

Dwarf Green Curled (60 days to maturity). A very pretty kale sometimes used as an ornamental plant, Dwarf Green Curled Kale has densely curled, frilly dark green leaves and can flourish in wet soils in harsh weather. The tender leaves can be harvested all winter. It is also known as Dwarf Curlies or Scotch Kale.

Dwarf Siberian (65 days to maturity). An extremely hardy plant with blue-gray plume-like leaves with slightly ruffled edges, Dwarf Siberian Kale grows well in both cold and warm climates.

Hanover Salad (60 to 75 days to maturity). This Siberian kale has smooth leaves with slightly scalloped edges and stems that can range in color from white to purple. Hanover Salad thrives in cooler temperatures and is also known as Early Hanover, Spring Kale, and Premier Kale.

Improved Dwarf Siberian (35 to 40 days to maturity). Often used as a baby leaf lettuce, this kale is a deep green color with smooth oval leaves and a slightly rippled edge.

Lacinato (60 to 62 days to maturity). This Italian heirloom kale has a primitive look with dark blue-green strap-like leaves that look puckered and can reach four inches wide and two feet long. Mild tasting and best eaten when smaller, Lacinato can hold up well in the heat but is also very cold hardy. It is also known as Lacinato Blue, Tuscan, Black Kale, Black Cabbage, Nero di Toscana, Cavolo Nero, Black Palm Tree, Tuscan Black Cabbage, and Dinosaur Kale.

Redbor (55 to 65 days to maturity). A glorious magenta kale with curly leaves, Redbor is often used in landscaping. The leaves are not just beautiful but also tender and mild tasting, almost sweet, especially after the first frost.

Red Russian (40 to 60 days to maturity). Russian traders brought this vigorous plant from Siberia to North America in the 1880s. Red Russian Kale has frilly, oak-shaped leaves that range in color from gray-green to purplish-red, and their color intensifies in cold weather. The stems and veins are often a deep purple. This kale is characterized by very tender leaves, and it can last through winter in temperatures as low as 0°F, producing again in the spring. It is also known as Ragged Jack and Russian Red.

Red Ursa (65 to 70 days to maturity). A cross between True Siberian and Red Russian Kale, Red Ursa possesses characteristics of each. The leaves can be flat to lushly frilled and have dramatic purple veins and stems with blue-green leaves. This kale is cold-weather hardy as well as heat tolerant.

Squire (60 days to maturity). An heirloom plant with extremely curly blue-green leaves that are very tender, Squire can hold very well all winter. The frost even improves its flavor.

True Siberian (70 days to maturity). The leaves of this plant are big, blue-green, and finely ruffled. True Siberian Kale is hardy in cold weather, and its flavor will improve after the first frost. You can pick it all winter in areas that are more temperate.

Vates Blue Curled (55 days to maturity). This is a wonderful container-garden kale because it is smaller than most kale and grows upright rather than spreading out. The leaves are blue-green and finely curled with sturdy stems. Vates Blue Curled Kale can be harvested in the winter and is cold hardy.

Winterbor (60 to 65 days to maturity). A lovely blue-green, finely curled kale that grows upright and tall, to three feet, Winterbor is winter hardy.

Winter Red (50 days to maturity). The red leaves of this kale resemble oak leaves with red veins and wavy edges. Winter Red is sweet even before the first frost, and the baby leaves can be harvested as soon as 25 days after seeding.

HOW TO SELECT GOOD KALE

Your recipes are only as good as the ingredients you use, so it is crucial to select the best kale possible. Although kale looks like a hardier member of the greens family, it requires some special handling to ensure its flavor and freshness. Kale is available year-round but is a winter crop. The best kale is available from the beginning of winter to early spring. Consider purchasing organic kale whenever possible, because nonorganically grown kale is on the Environmental Working Group's "Dirty Dozen" list (see page 241). This list, updated yearly, denotes which commercial produce crops are highest in pesticide contamination.

If you shop where greens are not stored in a cool display case, find another location to buy kale. Kale wilts in warm temperatures and develops an unpleasant bitter taste. Whenever possible, buy kale as an entire head, not chopped and sold in plastic containers. You want to be able to touch the greens to ascertain their firmness and check for browning, yellowing, or tiny holes in the leaves. Look for kale with smaller leaves for a more tender texture and milder flavor. If the kale is a lovely dark green with firm leaves and strong stems, take it home to star in all your recipes.

When you get home from the store, wash your kale and dry it *thoroughly*. Keep it stored in the refrigerator in a sealed plastic bag with all the air pressed out. Kale will last in the refrigerator up to two weeks if stored correctly, and it can be refreshed in a bowl of very cold water before using. Do not place kale near fruit that releases ethylene naturally, such as apples, avocados, melons, figs, stone fruit, tomatoes, and pears, because the kale will turn limp and yellow quickly. Wash the kale right before you prepare it, and do your best to enjoy this superfood at its peak flavor and texture.

NEED-TO-KNOW NUTRITION

Kale is a powerhouse food, and many benefits are associated with regularly including it in your meals. Kale is nutrient-dense, which means even small amounts can provide impressive quantities of essential vitamins, minerals, antioxidants, and macronutrients. One cup of kale (steamed or raw) is:

» *Higher in calcium per calorie than an 8-ounce glass of milk.* The calcium in kale is absorbed more easily because kale is also an excellent source of magnesium, which is needed for calcium absorption in the body.

» *A better source of vitamin C than a whole orange.* One cup of kale offers 134 percent of the recommended daily allowance, whereas an orange provides 113 percent. If you consider weight as well, kale has double the vitamin C of oranges, as one cup of kale weighs, on average, about 67 grams, and one orange weighs about 130 grams. One cup of kale also contains over 1,000 percent more vitamin C than spinach and has lower oxalate content, so the vitamin C is better absorbed.

» *An excellent source of amino acids.* Kale contains all the essential amino acids plus nine additional ones.

» *Very low in fat.* What little fat kale contains is mainly healthy omega-3 fatty acid. Kale is higher in omega-3 fatty acid (alpha-linolenic acid or ALA) than omega-6, which is a very rare ratio in most foods. One cup of kale provides 120 milligrams of omega-3 fatty acid, which can reduce your risk of type 2 diabetes and heart disease.

» *More iron rich than beef.* Comparing kale to beef calorie for calorie, kale yields a higher iron contribution to your diet.

» *Good for your cholesterol.* Cholesterol-free, steamed kale binds 42 percent more bile acid than a prescription drug called cholestyramine that is prescribed to lower cholesterol.

» *Very high in antioxidants.* Simple kale includes more than 45 antioxidants, including beta carotene, kaempferol, and quercetin.

» *A power boost of vitamin K.* Kale offers a whopping 1,180 percent of the recommended daily amount of vitamin K, about 550 milligrams.

» *Fiber rich.* Kale offers five times the fiber of fiber-rich oatmeal, when compared calorie for calorie.

TREND OR TIMELESS?

Kale is a tasty superfood that has recently taken over the Internet, restaurants, and, to some extent, home kitchens because it has become trendy to eat this healthy, nutrient-packed vegetable. One could simply dismiss kale as a food trend, but people have been cultivating and eating kale for more than 6,000 years. Although kale has made a more recent climb to popularity in North America, it has been enjoyed in many other cultures for centuries. In the Netherlands, a popular dish called *boerenkool* is made with mashed potatoes and finely chopped kale. In Germany, an annual celebration called *Grünkohlfahrt* is dedicated to eating kale. Kale is versatile and nutritious, and its long, rich history suggests it is here to stay.

Tips for Prep and Storing

Have you ever purchased a perky, new-spangled bunch of greens and found a limp, dull mess after storing them for a bit in your refrigerator? This decay is frustrating, and can be expensive when you toss out the greens in disgust. Kale can deteriorate into this unappetizing state if you don't prepare and store it correctly. The process can take a little time, but you will find it worthwhile when you have fresh, beautiful greens for your recipes.

PREPPING

Wash the kale thoroughly. Make sure you have a big enough container and enough water so the kale floats about three inches off the bottom. Submerge the kale leaves, swishing them around. As you wash the kale, the dirt will sink to the bottom of the container. Rinse each leaf under the tap, and shake off the excess water.

You can also stem the kale while you rinse it. First, hold the stem at the bottom of the leaf. Then, using the thumb and index finger of your other hand, make a ring around the stem right above where you are holding the leaf. Pull the entire leaf through the ring to strip the leafy part right off the tough stem. If this method doesn't work for you, you can use a sharp knife to de-rib the leaves. Fold the leaf over along the stem and cut the leaf section away from the tough stem.

When you have stemmed all the leaves, it's time to dry them. You won't want to skip this step. A salad spinner is the most effective tool for this task. If you do not have a spinner, clean kitchen towels will do the trick. Lay several clean kitchen towels flat, and scatter the rinsed and stemmed leaves in a single layer on the towels. Top with another clean towel, and roll the towels like a jelly roll. Fold the roll in half and press down so the towels absorb the liquid. Unroll the towels, and repeat until the kale is dry.

STORING

You can use the kale immediately after washing and drying it, but if you need to store it, it's important to pack it correctly. The trick to perfect kale is to keep it dry and well wrapped. Wet kale can rot and get slimy. Stack two paper towels on a flat surface, and place a few dried kale leaves on the end of the towels closest to you. Roll the end away from you, wrapping the kale leaves in the towel. When the kale leaves are enclosed, add more leaves along the width of the towel and roll up that kale as well. Repeat this process until the entire length of the towel is used up, and start again with two more paper towels until all your kale is wrapped.

Slide the rolled-up kale into large zip-top freezer bags, squeeze the air out, and seal. Store the bags in the vegetable crisper. The kale should stay fresh and crisp for up to two weeks, if you don't eat it all before then.

Do *not* chop the kale before storing it in the refrigerator, as doing so can diminish the nutrient value. If you want to freeze the kale, tear the leaves into pieces and scatter them on a baking tray. Place the tray in the freezer for about two hours, or until the kale is frozen. Transfer the frozen kale pieces to large zip-top bags and squeeze out as much air as possible without crushing the leaves. Seal the bags and place them in the freezer until you need the kale. Kale will keep for up to one month in the freezer, and you can throw it into soups and stews without thawing it.

Kale Myths: How Super Is It?

Kale has reached the zenith of food popularity and, as is often the case, negative press has emerged to knock this vegetable off its pedestal. There is no denying the incredible array of health benefits kale offers for those who eat it regularly. But is kale really as wonderful as its hype suggests, or are the anti-kale rumors true? Let's take a look.

Kale is too expensive. In 2011, kale was a staple item in just under 5,000 stores. By 2014, it was sold in just under 51,000 stores. Sometimes this type of volume increase results from a food becoming less expensive. In the case of kale, however, the price has increased by 25 percent over the same time frame. So while kale has become more expensive, the question to ask is whether it is too expensive to include in your meals.

The answer is no. Kale has increased a little more than the average vegetable's price in the same time frame, about 15 percent, but it is not priced out of sight. A bunch of kale costs around $2.00, on average, and a bunch is generally huge. You can make a week's worth of smoothies or several salads using one bunch. Kale remains one of the most inexpensive vegetable choices, and the comparison between money spent and the return on your health makes kale infinitely affordable.

Kale can cause hypothyroidism. This idea arose because kale is a cruciferous vegetable that is a rich source of glucosinolates. This compound creates a substance (called goitrin) that can interfere with the thyroid's iodine uptake, causing an enlargement of that gland. As a result, kale can be considered a "goitrogenic" food, and the current argument is that eating kale in excess can cause hypothyroidism.

This argument was bolstered by Oregon State University's Micronutrient Information Center, which outlined a reported case of an 88-year-old woman who consumed 1 to 1.5 kilograms (about 3.3 pounds) of raw bok choy per day for several months and ended up in a coma with severe hypothyroidism. Even overlooking the fact you would have to eat about 15 cups of kale to equal that amount, a person would also have to have an iodine deficiency to create thyroid issues.

Iodine deficiency has been almost unheard of in the United States since the introduction of iodized salt in the 1920s. If you do not suffer from thyroid issues to begin with, eating kale regularly in generous amounts is not going to cause hypothyroidism. If you do have thyroid issues, it is prudent to follow your doctor's recommendations with respect to all cruciferous vegetables.

Kale can cause kidney stones. Kale contains oxalic acid, which can cause health issues such as kidney stones because it can crystallize when too concentrated in body fluids. Oxalic acid has also been shown to bind calcium in the intestines, lowering the availability of this mineral to the body. The important consideration here is that the amount of calcium in kale is very high, and the decrease in its availability for the body's use from the oxalic acid is low. So, if you decide not to eat kale because you think it will deplete calcium from your system, consider that the amount of calcium you do get by eating it is substantially more than the tiny amount not available due to the oxalic acid. It is a very good trade-off.

KALE POWDER? KALE SUPPLEMENTS?

Eating fresh kale is the best choice when considering the health benefits and taste, but you might not always have access to high-quality, fresh kale. Kale supplements and powder can be a good option for getting kale into your diet. The supplements are available in capsules, and the recommended dosage is about 100 to 350 milligrams per day. You can also get dried kale leaves to make into tea.

Kale powder is very easy to make if you have dried kale and a blender. You can either dry the kale in a dehydrator or massage kale leaves with olive oil and crisp them in a 350°F oven for about 15 minutes. Pulse the completely dried and cooled kale leaves in a blender or food processor until very powdery, for about three minutes. Store the powder in an airtight glass container for up to two weeks. Use the powder in smoothies, salads, pasta, oatmeal, and entrées.

Kale is also extremely rich in most other nutrients, so the decrease in calcium should be weighed against that benefit, too. The body can rid itself of high amounts of oxalic acid, unless one is genetically predisposed to an inability to process it. People with gallbladder issues, rheumatoid arthritis, and kidney disorders should avoid kale, but a healthy person developing kidney stones from eating kale is highly unlikely.

Kale is contaminated with pesticides. This assertion is both true and untrue, according to the Environmental Working Group (EWG) in their 2014 report, *Shopper's Guide to Pesticides in Produce.* Kale did not make the "Dirty Dozen" list, but it was included in the Dirty Dozen PLUS, along with collard greens and hot peppers. Commercially grown kale is contaminated by a pesticide that is highly toxic to the nervous system (organophosphate insecticide) but is not completely coated in a plethora of different pesticides. If you wish to avoid the health-related risks of eating pesticide-contaminated foods, buy organic kale or grow your own. Wash your kale thoroughly no matter where you get this vegetable to remove the residue of any substance.

KALE FOR EVERYONE

The recipes in this book are clearly labeled to help you choose dishes that suit your specific needs, diet, and tastes—and available time and energy. As you scan the recipes, you'll quickly see the information you need without having to search through all the ingredient lists. The following labels are included to help you feed almost any type of eater, on just about any type of day:

KIDS: Children—notoriously picky eaters—often turn their noses up at many vegetables, including kale. The palate can be trained to like or dislike foods through familiarity and simple preference for ingredients that taste a certain way, such as sweet. Introducing kids to kale, or making it a part of their daily diet, is a good way to create healthy lifestyle habits. You can certainly hide kale in recipes, such as puréed in baked goods or blended into smoothies, but creating a true appreciation for the taste, texture, and appearance of this spectacular green is a better option. The recipes considered kid-friendly in this book are family favorites, familiar dishes like pizza, and other fun or interesting recipes.

MEAT LOVERS: Finding dishes that appeal to meat lovers in a book devoted to kale might seem like a long shot, but there are many recipes here that have enough meat in them to satisfy a dedicated carnivore. Whole chicken breasts or thighs, thick venison and beef stews, meaty pork chops, and juicy turkey breasts are all enhanced by a healthy amount of fresh kale. You will come to appreciate that, even if your preference is meat in all its forms, you can still get heaps of nutrients by adding a versatile green like kale to your favorite recipes.

VEGANS: The vegan diet excludes all animal products, thus adding kale is spectacularly simple; if you're already following this diet, you're likely already including heaps of greens in many meals. If not, kale is a nice way to start because it is quite forgiving to cook. Kale has a heartier texture than spinach, so it can take those few extra minutes in a pot or skillet without totally disintegrating. Vegan diets are not necessarily healthy diets because processed fatty foods can still be vegan, so kale is a good way to get the required nutrition for essential body functions. People follow a vegan diet for many reasons other than their health, such as ethical and environmental concerns. The vegan recipes in this book exclude:

→ Meat and animal by-products (including fish, shellfish, poultry, gelatin, and rennet)
→ Dairy (including milk, cheese, and yogurt)
→ Eggs
→ Honey

PALEOS: Although the Paleo diet is often referred to as the "caveman diet," vegetables, including greens like kale, are a crucial part of the plan. The Paleo diet is very popular and based on the premise that modern people are less healthy than our ancestors because of today's commonly eaten foods.

Foods included on the Paleo plan center around ingredients that hunter-gatherers would source instead of agriculture-based products, such as refined sugars, dairy, grains, salt, and processed foods. Kale falls squarely in the "unprocessed" category and can easily be combined with other Paleo ingredients to create amazing dishes. The recipes labeled "Paleos" in this book do not include:

- » Cereal grains
- » Dairy
- » Excessively salty foods
- » Legumes
- » Potatoes
- » Processed foods
- » Refined sugar
- » Refined vegetable oils

GLUTEN-FREES: People following gluten-free diets usually have celiac disease or are sensitive to gluten. Gluten is a protein in wheat, barley, and rye. If a person has celiac, gluten can damage the small intestine and inhibit the absorption of nutrients. This condition causes uncomfortable symptoms that can be controlled by avoiding gluten. The recipes in this book labeled for "Gluten-Frees" do not contain wheat, barley, rye, or products that contain these foods.

LARGE GROUPS: Sometimes you need to prepare large amounts of food for an event, and finding recipes that double and even triple well can be difficult. Some ingredients, such as salt, garlic, flour, and spices, don't perform well in larger amounts when recipes are scaled for increased servings. The recipes here appropriate for large groups serve more than six and can be made in greater quantities with no change in flavor or texture. These recipes include casseroles, stews, ice pops, salads, and soups.

SINGLETONS: Making homemade meals when it is just you can be challenging, as most recipes are designed to serve at least four people. This can leave you with leftovers that don't keep well or dishes that flop because scaling them down doesn't work. If you see recipes marked "Singletons," you'll

know the dish will make smaller amounts, or the recipe keeps or freezes well for several days of leftovers.

30-MINUTE: In today's fast-paced, schedule-heavy society, it can be impossible to carve out time to make wholesome meals for your family. Having a few speedy meals in your culinary repertoire can relieve stress and free up the time you need for other commitments. The "30-minute" recipes take 30 minutes from walking into the kitchen to sitting down to chow. Some recipes, such as the ice pops, require additional time for freezing.

ONE POT: Creating kitchen chaos with an assortment of pots, pans, and bowls can make cooking less than attractive for many people. Complicated recipes often produce stellar meals, but the idea of a meal made in one pot or bowl is very alluring. One-pot recipes in this book do not include smoothies or juices, which are technically produced without extras beyond a blender or juicer. "One-Pot" meals are constructed in a single skillet, saucepan, bowl, baking dish, or stockpot.

MAKE AHEAD: Recipes that can hold in the refrigerator or freeze well are perfect to make ahead for mealtimes with little muss or fuss. These recipes can be prepared during a batch cooking session, such as when making casseroles, soups, or stews. "Make-ahead" recipes can also be prepared ahead and put in the oven the next day. These include stuffed squash, potato skins, and fish packets. You'll also see some salads and other dishes that benefit from time to marinate or freeze.

Kale
a timeline

The exact origins of kale are unclear, but it is thought that the cruciferous vegetable we enjoy today came from the wild cabbage found in Asia Minor in prehistoric times. Fossilized impressions of leaves bearing a resemblance to today's kale have been found in this region. Let's take a look back on kale's history:

600 BC
Kale is thought to have made its way to Europe with Celtic people. From then on, there are references to kale, or what is most likely kale, in historical records.

234 to 149 BC
The health benefits of the entire Brassica family are written about by Cato "the Censor," who recommends that cooking or pickling this vegetable is the best choice.

500 to 1500
Kale becomes so popular in the Middle Ages in Scotland and England that the word "kale" means "dinner."

4000 BC
In Shensi Province, China, fossilized evidence indicates that ancient ceramic containers held kale-like leaves.

4000 BC

5th century BC
The vegetable known as kale today is developed and called the "cabbage of the vegetable garden without a head."

371 BC to 287 BC
The father of botany, Theophrastus, mentions in his writings a nonheading curly-leaved cabbage that was different from wild cabbage.

2012
Bon Appétit names 2012 the Year of Kale. Additionally, 2,500 farms are harvesting kale in the United States, up from fewer than 1,000 in 2007.

2013
October 2 is the first annual National Kale Day. Kale is searched 18.2 million times this year on Google, nine times as many searches as in 2012.

World War II
Home gardeners are advised to grow kale for the "Dig for Victory" campaign.

1620
Kale is used in the kitchens in Versailles.

2014 AD

1300 to 1700
During the Renaissance, Italian botanists create "Tuscan" kale.

19th century
In the local Scottish dialect, "kail" means "food" in general.

2014
Kale scores at the top of the Whole Foods Market nutrition rating system called ANDI, an acronym for Aggregate Nutrient Density Index, created by Dr. Joel Fuhrman, the author of *Eat to Live*. Kale scores 1,000 on the 1 to 1,000 scale, along with mustard greens, turnip greens, collard greens, Swiss chard, and watercress.

2

The Very Basics

Broiled Kale

SERVES 4 / PREP: 5 MINUTES / COOK: 10 MINUTES / TOTAL: 15 MINUTES

This method of preparing kale creates a lovely, unique side dish for red meats, poultry, and wild game. The texture is both crispy and soft because the edges of the kale crisp in the heat, leaving the inner parts of the leaves still wilted and tender. A little sprinkle of salt and pepper is all that is needed to finish this dish, but you can go bold with other spices and herbs to suit your palate and the other components of your meal.

6 cups stemmed and chopped kale
1 tablespoon extra-virgin olive oil, divided
Sea salt
Freshly ground black pepper

Preheat the oven to broil. Put the top oven rack in the upper third of the oven.

Top a baking sheet with a wire rack. Spread about 3 cups of kale out on the rack, avoiding too much overlap.

Drizzle the kale with 1½ teaspoons of olive oil, and season with sea salt and pepper.

Broil the kale for about 4 minutes, or until the edges are crispy.

Remove the baking sheet from the oven and transfer the kale to a large serving bowl.

Repeat with the remaining 3 cups of kale, the remaining 1½ teaspoons of olive oil, and the sea salt and pepper. Serve immediately.

Per Serving Calories: 80; Total Fat: 4g; Sodium: 102mg; Protein: 3g

Blanched Kale

VEGANS, PALEOS, GLUTEN-FREES, LARGE GROUPS, SINGLETONS, 30-MINUTE, ONE POT, MAKE AHEAD

SERVES 4 / PREP: 10 MINUTES / COOK: 5 MINUTES / TOTAL: 15 MINUTES

Double or triple this recipe so you always have blanched kale on hand, as it is an invaluable ingredient for many recipes. Use it right from the blanching pot or freeze it for future meals. If you freeze the kale, blanching is crucial: The boiling water and water bath process will destroy the enzymes that make kale bitter.

Pinch sea salt
7 cups stemmed and chopped kale

Fill a large pot with water. Place it over high heat, add the sea salt, and bring to a boil.

Add the kale to the pot, cover, and blanch for 2 to 3 minutes, or until it turns bright green.

Drain the kale, and run it under cold water until completely cooled.

Squeeze out the excess liquid, and pat dry. If not using immediately, transfer the kale to a resealable plastic bag and refrigerate for up to 2 days.

Tip **The trick to perfect frozen blanched kale is to dry it completely before placing it into the resealable bags. Spin the blanched greens in a salad spinner, and then scatter the mostly dry leaves on a clean kitchen towel. Roll the towel like a jelly roll and squeeze. Then, place the dried kale on a parchment-lined baking sheet in a single layer and freeze for 30 minutes. Transfer the frozen leaves to the resealable bags, store in the freezer, and remove the kale in handfuls as you need it.**

Per Serving Calories: 56; Total Fat: 0g; Sodium: 78mg; Protein: 3g

Sautéed Kale

VEGANS, PALEOS, GLUTEN-FREES, LARGE GROUPS, SINGLETONS, 30-MINUTE, ONE POT

SERVES 4 / PREP: 5 MINUTES / COOK: 10 MINUTES / TOTAL: 15 MINUTES

You might be surprised at the volume of kale in the sauté pan at the beginning of the cooking time. No need to worry; the greens will wilt quickly as you toss them over the heat. You can season this dish in any way that strikes your fancy, but salt and pepper with a quick squeeze of fresh lemon juice to brighten the flavor is delicious.

2 tablespoons extra-virgin olive oil
7 cups stemmed and coarsely chopped kale
Sea salt
Freshly ground black pepper
1 tablespoon freshly squeezed lemon juice

In a large skillet over medium-high heat, heat the olive oil.

Add the kale and begin tossing with tongs. As the kale wilts, continue tossing to move any raw kale to the heat.

When all the kale is wilted and tender, after about 10 minutes, remove it from the heat.

Season with salt, pepper, and lemon juice, and toss together. Serve hot.

Per Serving Calories: 86; Total Fat: 4g; Sodium: 108mg; Protein: 3g

Braised Kale

SERVES 4 / PREP: 10 MINUTES / COOK: 30 MINUTES / TOTAL: 40 MINUTES

Braising uses both dry and moist heat to create tender greens, vegetables, and meats. Food is first pan-seared and then finished in liquid to enhance the flavor. Whatever liquid you use will infuse the kale, so experiment with broth, herbs, and accents, such as soy sauce, to create the perfect dish.

1 tablespoon extra-virgin olive oil
1 sweet onion, thinly sliced
½ teaspoon sea salt
¼ teaspoon freshly ground black pepper
10 cups stemmed and chopped kale
1 tablespoon minced garlic
1 cup chicken broth

In a large skillet over high heat, heat the olive oil.

Add the onion, and sauté for 2 minutes. Season with sea salt and pepper.

Add the kale and garlic to the skillet. Lightly sear the kale, tossing with tongs for about 4 minutes.

Add the chicken broth, and bring the liquid to a boil, tossing the kale until completely wilted.

Reduce the heat to medium, and braise the kale for 15 to 20 minutes, or until very tender.

Remove from the heat and serve.

Per Serving Calories: 126; Total Fat: 4g; Sodium: 556mg; Protein: 5g

Boiled Kale

VEGANS, PALEOS, GLUTEN-FREES, LARGE GROUPS, SINGLETONS, 30-MINUTE, ONE POT, MAKE AHEAD

SERVES 4 / PREP: 5 MINUTES / COOK: 25 MINUTES / TOTAL: 30 MINUTES

Boiling is not the most popular cooking technique when it comes to preparing kale, but it can be a good method when using larger leaves in recipes. Boiling will tenderize those tougher leaves. Be sure to keep the kale water for soups, as it contains many antioxidants and nutrients.

2 cups water
¼ teaspoon sea salt
7 cups stemmed and coarsely chopped kale

In a large pot over high heat, bring the water and sea salt to a boil.

Add the kale to the pot, and reduce the heat to low. Simmer the kale for 20 to 25 minutes, or until tender.

Drain and serve.

Per Serving Calories: 56; Total Fat: 0g; Sodium: 166mg; Protein: 3g

Panfried Kale

VEGANS, PALEOS, GLUTEN-FREES, LARGE GROUPS, SINGLETONS, 30-MINUTE, ONE POT

SERVES 4 / PREP: 5 MINUTES / COOK: 5 MINUTES / TOTAL: 10 MINUTES

Although the star of this dish is the kale, you can change up the flavor using different infused olive oils, nut oils, or other favorites. Roasted garlic oil, basil oil, chili pepper oil, and tarragon oil are all lovely with kale, as are sesame and walnut oils. Regardless of which you choose, do not use too much oil, or the kale will be soggy and greasy rather than tender with a crispy edge.

1 tablespoon extra-virgin olive oil
1 tablespoon minced garlic
10 cups stemmed and chopped kale
Sea salt
Freshly ground black pepper

In a large skillet over medium-high heat, heat the olive oil.

Add the garlic, and sauté for about 2 minutes, or until softened.

Add the kale, and season lightly with sea salt and pepper.

Toss the kale with tongs until wilted, but still slightly crisp, about 3 minutes.

Remove from the heat and serve.

Per Serving Calories: 116; Total Fat: 4g; Sodium: 131mg; Protein: 5g

Steamed Kale

Steaming kale can be an ideal method of cooking this superfood because the fiber component of kale binds bile acids better when steamed. This means the cholesterol-lowering abilities of this potent green are enhanced, resulting in better "bad" (LDL) cholesterol numbers at your next doctor's checkup.

2 teaspoons extra-virgin olive oil
1 teaspoon minced garlic
8 cups stemmed and chopped kale
⅔ cup water or chicken broth
Sea salt
1 tablespoon balsamic vinegar or
   apple cider vinegar

In a deep skillet over medium-high heat, heat the olive oil.

Add the garlic, and sauté for about 2 minutes, or until tender.

Add the kale. Using tongs, toss for about 2 minutes, or until the volume of the leaves is reduced by three-fourths.

Add the water and sea salt, and bring to a boil.

Reduce the heat to medium, cover, and simmer for about 20 minutes, or until the kale is very tender.

Stir in the vinegar, and serve.

Tip If you have a steamer, this process is even simpler. Fill the bottom of a steamer with 3 inches of water, and bring to a boil. Add the kale to the steamer basket, cover, and steam the kale for 5 minutes. Remove the greens from the steamer, and season lightly with sea salt and pepper.

Per Serving Calories: 88; Total Fat: 2g; Sodium: 118mg; Protein: 4g

Grilled Kale

KIDS, VEGANS, PALEOS, GLUTEN-FREES, SINGLETONS, 30-MINUTE, ONE POT

SERVES 4 / PREP: 10 MINUTES / COOK: 5 MINUTES / TOTAL: 15 MINUTES

Barbecuing has become a culinary art form, complete with TV shows and cookbooks devoted to proper technique and interesting ingredients. Kale grills up nicely because the leaves hold up well under higher heat—and crisp rather than char. The trick to perfect grilled kale is massaging oil into every crevice so the kale does not burn or soften.

½ cup extra-virgin olive oil
1 tablespoon freshly squeezed lemon juice
1 teaspoon minced garlic
2 bunches kale, stemmed
Sea salt
Freshly ground black pepper

Preheat the grill or a grill pan to medium-high heat.

In a large bowl, whisk together the olive oil, lemon juice, and garlic.

Add the kale leaves to the bowl, and toss until well coated.

Season lightly with sea salt and pepper.

Lay the kale leaves in a single layer on the preheated grill. Cook for 1 to 2 minutes, or until crispy.

Turn the leaves, and grill the other side for 1 minute more.

Serve immediately.

Per Serving Calories: 274; Total Fat: 25g; Sodium: 108mg; Protein: 3g

Creamed Kale

There is something comforting about creamed vegetables. They evoke memories of childhood and festive events where huge tureens graced the tables. If you want a less calorie-laden version, use evaporated milk instead of heavy cream. A vegan version can also be created by swapping out the butter for olive oil, the chicken broth for vegetable broth, and the cream for coconut milk.

1 tablespoon unsalted butter
½ sweet onion, thinly sliced
3½ cups stemmed and coarsely chopped kale
½ cup chicken broth
¼ cup heavy cream
Pinch sea salt
Pinch freshly ground black pepper
Pinch ground nutmeg

In a large skillet over medium heat, melt the butter.

Add the onion, and sauté for about 6 minutes, or until lightly caramelized.

Stir in the kale, chicken broth, heavy cream, sea salt, pepper, and nutmeg. Continue stirring until the kale wilts.

Cook for about 20 minutes, stirring occasionally, until the cream is thickened and the kale is tender.

Serve immediately.

Per Serving Calories: 81; Total Fat: 5g; Sodium: 202mg; Protein: 2g

Pickled Kale

MAKES 2 QUARTS / PREP: 10 MINUTES / COOK: 10 MINUTES / TOTAL: 2 DAYS, 20 MINUTES

Pickling is an ancient method of preserving foods that works beautifully with greens. You may not have tried pickled greens before, but the tender-crisp texture and delightful tangy-sweet flavor will surely make you a fan. Jazz up your pickled kale with herb sprigs, crushed garlic cloves, fresh ginger pieces, or hot peppers.

4 cups filtered water
1¼ cups sugar
1 cup white vinegar
1 tablespoon kosher salt
2 teaspoons black peppercorns
7 cups stemmed and coarsely chopped kale

In a large pot over high heat, bring the water, sugar, vinegar, kosher salt, and black peppercorns to a boil. Reduce the heat to low, and simmer for 5 minutes.

Add the kale, and continue to simmer for about 2 minutes, or until the kale wilts slightly.

Remove the pot from the heat, and let the kale cool completely.

Pack the kale into sterilized 1-quart jars.

Pour the leftover liquid into the jars so it reaches to about 1 inch below the rims. Cover with the sterilized lids and secure tightly.

Refrigerate the jars for at least 2 days before serving. The pickled kale can be kept, refrigerated, for up to 1 week. If unopened, it will keep for 2 weeks.

Tip Many people avoid pickling because they think the process of sterilizing the jars is tedious and hard to manage. If you have a dishwasher, check to see if there is a sanitizing cycle. You can also preheat the oven to 225°F, put the jars and lids in a pan, and heat in the oven for 20 minutes.

Per Serving (1 cup) Calories: 153; Total Fat: 0g; Sodium: 898mg; Protein: 2g

Citrus Sauce

KIDS, VEGANS, PALEOS, GLUTEN-FREES, LARGE GROUPS, SINGLETONS, 30-MINUTE, ONE POT, MAKE AHEAD

MAKES 1 CUP / PREP: 10 MINUTES / TOTAL: 10 MINUTES

Oranges and lemons are ranked as the most-consumed fruits in the world. Both provide extensive support for the immune system and are very high in vitamin C. Just one orange contains the minimum recommended daily amount of vitamin C for an adult. Lemons are also nutritional powerhouses that can help the body fight infections, detoxify, and treat digestive concerns, such as heartburn.

½ cup extra-virgin olive oil
Juice of ½ lemon
3 tablespoons freshly squeezed orange juice
1 scallion, minced
Zest of ½ lemon
Zest of 1 orange
½ orange, peeled and chopped coarsely
¼ jalapeño pepper, minced
1 teaspoon minced fresh thyme

In a small bowl, whisk together the olive oil, lemon juice, and orange juice until well blended.

Whisk in the scallion, lemon zest, orange zest, orange, jalapeño, and thyme.

Refrigerate in a sealed container for up to 1 week.

Tip **Always wash citrus carefully using a soft-bristle brush and mild soapy water to remove any pesticide residues, even if you buy organic fruit. Some organic and commercially grown citrus fruits are coated with wax to protect the skin during transport. Be sure to scrub that layer off before zesting for the recipe.**

Per Serving (2 tablespoons) Calories: 119; Total Fat: 13g; Sodium: 0mg; Protein: 0g

Hollandaise Sauce

KIDS, PALEOS, GLUTEN-FREES

MAKES 1 CUP / PREP: 20 MINUTES / COOK: 10 MINUTES + 15 MINUTES TO COOL / TOTAL: 45 MINUTES

Imagine a luscious, silky, buttery sauce spooned over tender, vibrant green sautéed kale, and you might be thinking of hollandaise. This is a sauce that must be created à la minute (right before serving), as it will not hold in the refrigerator for days. You will need a good whisk, patience, and perfectly clarified butter to make hollandaise. Just follow this recipe, and soon you will have a perfect sauce that any chef would be proud of for your kale.

For the clarified butter
¾ cup (1½ sticks) unsalted butter

For the finished sauce
2 egg yolks
1 teaspoon cold water
2 teaspoons freshly squeezed lemon juice, divided
Pinch sea salt

To make the clarified butter:
In a medium, heavy-bottomed saucepan over low heat, slowly melt the butter. Remove the pan from the heat, and let the butter stand for 5 minutes. Using a spoon, skim off any foam.

Pour the clear yellow clarified butter into a container, without adding any of the milky solids in the bottom of the pan. Discard the milky solids. Cool the clarified butter for 15 minutes.

To make the finished sauce:
In a small saucepan over medium heat, add about 2 inches of water and heat to a simmer.

In a medium stainless-steel bowl, whisk together the egg yolks and cold water for about 3 minutes, or until foamy and light.

Whisk in ¼ teaspoon of lemon juice.

Set the bowl on the saucepan over the simmering water, making sure the bottom of the bowl does not touch the water.

Whisk the yolks for about 2 minutes, or until they thicken a little. Remove the bowl from over the saucepan.

▸⟶

Hollandaise Sauce, continued

Pour the clarified butter slowly, in a very thin stream, into the yolk mixture, whisking continuously, until all the butter is used and the sauce is thick and smooth.

Whisk in the remaining 1¾ teaspoons of lemon juice.

Season with sea salt, and serve immediately.

 Tip This sauce should be used within 1 hour, and any excess should be discarded.

Per Serving (1 tablespoon) Calories: 83; Total Fat: 9g; Sodium: 78mg; Protein: 1g

Peanut Sauce

KIDS, GLUTEN-FREES, LARGE GROUPS, SINGLETONS, 30-MINUTE, ONE POT, MAKE AHEAD

MAKES 1½ CUPS / PREP: 5 MINUTES / COOK: 0 / TOTAL: 5 MINUTES

Peanut butter is more than just a sandwich spread. In many countries it's used in soups and marinades, and as a crucial component in sauces. Peanut butter contains healthy unsaturated fat and is a rich source of dietary fiber, protein, and folate. Including this peanut sauce as an accompaniment to your kale dishes can improve your good cholesterol levels and help fight heart disease and cancer.

1 cup natural peanut butter
½ cup honey
¼ cup toasted sesame oil
¼ cup freshly squeezed lemon juice
2 tablespoons tahini
1 tablespoon soy sauce
½ teaspoon red pepper flakes
Water (if needed)

In a blender, process the peanut butter, honey, sesame oil, lemon juice, tahini, and soy sauce until very smooth.

Blend in the red pepper flakes, and thin the sauce with water if needed.

Store the sauce in a sealed container in the refrigerator for up to 1 week.

Per Serving (1 tablespoon) Calories: 117; Total Fat: 8g; Sodium: 42mg; Protein: 4g

Béarnaise Sauce

PALEOS, GLUTEN-FREES

MAKES 1 CUP / PREP: 10 MINUTES / COOK: 20 MINUTES + 15 MINUTES COOLING / TOTAL: 45 MINUTES

The herb in this velvety sauce might be unfamiliar because it is not often used in mainstream dishes in North America. Tarragon is a gorgeous licorice-tasting herb that should only be used fresh. When dried, this herb loses its essential oils, which means less flavor. However, if you have any leftover tarragon, you can easily freeze it. Pop whole sprigs into a resealable plastic bag, and use them another time right from the freezer.

For the clarified butter
¾ cup (1 ½ sticks) unsalted butter

For the finished sauce
¼ cup white wine vinegar
1 tablespoon chopped shallot
¼ teaspoon crushed black peppercorns
1 teaspoon chopped fresh tarragon, divided
2 large egg yolks
1 teaspoon chopped fresh parsley
Pinch sea salt
Squeeze of fresh lemon juice

To make the clarified butter:
In a medium, heavy-bottomed saucepan over low heat, melt the butter slowly. Remove the pan from the heat, and let the butter stand for 5 minutes. Using a spoon, skim off any foam.

Pour the clear yellow clarified butter into a container, being sure to avoid adding any of the milky solids in the bottom of the pan. Discard the milky solids. Let the clarified butter cool for 15 minutes.

To make the finished sauce:
In a small saucepan over medium-high heat, stir together the white wine vinegar, shallots, peppercorns, and ½ teaspoon of tarragon.

Bring the mixture to a simmer. Cook for about 3 minutes, or until reduced to 1 tablespoon of liquid.

In a medium stainless-steel bowl, combine the egg yolks and vinegar reduction. Whisk together for about 3 minutes, or until the mixture is foamy and light.

In a small saucepan over medium heat, heat about 2 inches of water to a simmer.

Set the bowl with the yolks on the saucepan over the simmering water, making sure the bottom of the bowl does not touch the water.

Whisk the yolk mixture for about 2 minutes, or until it thickens a little. Remove the bowl from over the simmering water.

Slowly pour the clarified butter into the yolk mixture, in a very thin stream, whisking continuously until all the butter is used and the sauce is thick and smooth.

Strain the sauce into a clean bowl. Stir in the remaining ½ teaspoon of tarragon and the parsley.

Season with sea salt and lemon juice.

 This sauce should be used within 1 hour, and any excess should be discarded.

Per Serving (1 tablespoon) Calories: 84; Total Fat: 9g; Sodium: 78mg; Protein: 1g

Aioli

MAKES 1 CUP / PREP: 10 MINUTES / COOK: 0 / TOTAL: 10 MINUTES

Aioli—a fancy word for garlic mayonnaise—is a combination of the French words for *garlic* and *oil*. When making this lush, richly flavored condiment, follow the recipe's instructions to use both canola oil and regular olive oil. The canola oil's milder flavor lets the taste of the remaining ingredients shine through. Don't use extra-virgin olive oil in this recipe, because it will cause the aioli to separate.

1 egg
1½ teaspoons Dijon mustard
1 teaspoon minced garlic
½ cup olive oil
½ cup canola oil
1 tablespoon freshly squeezed lemon juice
Sea salt

In a medium bowl, whisk together the egg, mustard, and garlic until well blended, about 2 minutes.

While whisking constantly, slowly add the olive oil in a thin, continuous stream.

Continue to whisk while slowly adding the canola oil in a thin, continuous stream, until the aioli is thick and emulsified.

Whisk in the lemon juice until blended.

Season with sea salt.

Refrigerate in an airtight container up to 4 days.

Tip For a truly sublime flavor, roast the garlic before adding it to the sauce. Put the peeled garlic cloves in an ovenproof skillet, and drizzle liberally with olive oil. Cover the skillet with foil, and bake at 350°F for about 15 minutes, or until the garlic is golden brown, softened, and fragrant.

Per Serving (1 tablespoon) Calories: 120; Total Fat: 13g; Sodium: 26mg; Protein: 0g

3

Smoothies
and Juices

Peachy Kale Smoothie

KIDS, VEGANS, PALEOS, GLUTEN-FREES, SINGLETONS, 30-MINUTE

SERVES 2 / PREP: 5 MINUTES / COOK: 0 / TOTAL: 5 MINUTES

The sweetness of peaches combines very well with kale and tart pomegranate to create this pastel-colored smoothie. Peaches support the immune system, the cardiovascular system, and vision health. This pretty stone fruit is packed with beta carotene, zinc, potassium, and vitamins A and C.

2 cups stemmed kale

1 frozen banana, cut into chunks

1 cup frozen peach slices

¾ cup 100% pomegranate juice, plus extra for thinning

½ cup water

½ cup almond milk

In a blender, blend the kale, banana, peach slices, pomegranate juice, water, and almond milk until the mixture is smooth.

Add more pomegranate juice, if needed, to thin the texture.

Serve immediately.

Tip When bananas reach that very ripe stage and the peel is covered with black spots, it's the perfect time to freeze them. Bananas can be frozen peel and all, but for the easiest smoothie prep, peel the bananas, cut them into chunks, then seal them in a plastic freezer bag or container. They will keep for several months.

Per Serving Calories: 204; Total Fat: 1g; Sodium: 81mg; Protein: 4g

Lemon-Thyme-Kale Smoothie

GLUTEN-FREES, SINGLETONS, 30-MINUTE

SERVES 2 / PREP: 5 MINUTES / COOK: 0 / TOTAL: 5 MINUTES

You will love the glorious color of this subtly green-flecked smoothie as well as the tart yet still-sweet taste. Pineapple is a superb complement to kale because its sweetness offsets any bitterness in the greens. It's also an excellent source of vitamins B_6, C, and E, as well as calcium, iron, and potassium. If you're feeling under the weather, whip up this smoothie. It can boost your immune system and improve digestive issues.

1 mango, peeled, pitted, and cut into chunks
1 banana, cut into chunks
1 cup pineapple chunks
1 cup stemmed kale
¼ cup water
4 tablespoons plain Greek yogurt
3 tablespoons freshly squeezed lemon juice
2 tablespoons chopped fresh thyme
4 ice cubes

In a blender, blend the mango, banana, pineapple, kale, water, yogurt, lemon juice, thyme, and ice until smooth.

Serve immediately.

Tip If you can't find a nice fresh, ripe mango, there are quality frozen and canned products you can use. Canned mango is easy to find in most grocery stores as well as many international markets, but confirm that the product is packed in juice, not sugar syrup.

Per Serving Calories: 214; Total Fat: 1g; Sodium: 29mg; Protein: 5g

Sunshine Orange–Kale Smoothie

KIDS, VEGANS, PALEOS, GLUTEN-FREES, SINGLETONS, 30-MINUTE

SERVES 2 / PREP: 10 MINUTES / COOK: 0 / TOTAL: 10 MINUTES

Simple ingredients create a delicious, nutritious smoothie combined with a healthy dose of kale. This drink is best for people who regularly include kale in their diet, as large amounts of raw kale can cause bloating and stomach issues for those who don't eat it regularly. If you still want to try this smoothie and are a kale amateur, reduce the greens to one cup.

1 cantaloupe, peeled, seeded, and cut into chunks
2 cups stemmed kale
½ cup freshly squeezed orange juice
3 ice cubes

In a blender, blend the cantaloupe, kale, orange juice, and ice until smooth.

Serve immediately.

Tip Selecting a ripe melon can often seem like a matter of luck. There are strategies you can use to ensure a sweet, juicy choice. If the melon feels heavier than it looks and makes a deep, dull noise when tapped, it is probably ripe. Also, press the spot where the melon was attached to the vine with your thumb; it should give a little.

Per Serving Calories: 117; Total Fat: 0g; Sodium: 70mg; Protein: 5g

Cherry-Berry-Kale Smoothie

KIDS, VEGANS, PALEOS, GLUTEN-FREES, SINGLETONS, 30-MINUTE

SERVES 2 / PREP: 5 MINUTES / COOK: 0 / TOTAL: 5 MINUTES

Black cherry juice can usually be found in the organic section of most major grocery stores or specialty health food stores. This juice is very beneficial for those who have problems with gout because just one cup can clear excess uric acid from the body in a few hours. Although kale is sometimes considered a food to avoid if you have gout, it is low in purine and packed full of beneficial nutrients.

3 cups stemmed kale
1 cup black cherries, pitted
1 cup frozen berries, any type
1 cup black cherry juice or apple juice
4 ice cubes

In a blender, process the kale, cherries, berries, cherry juice, and ice until smooth.

Serve immediately.

Tip **Black cherries are also available frozen and pitted, which can be very convenient and neater than pitting them yourself. Avoid canned or bottled cherries, as they are often packed in sugary syrup, which will add too many calories to your smoothie.**

Per Serving Calories: 208; Total Fat: 0g; Sodium: 57mg; Protein: 4g

Zesty Beet-Berry-Kale Smoothie

VEGANS, PALEOS, GLUTEN-FREES, SINGLETONS, 30-MINUTE

SERVES 2 / PREP: 10 MINUTES / COOK: 0 / TOTAL: 15 MINUTES

In this eye-pleasing as well as palate-pleasing smoothie, beets add an intense rosy color and an earthy sweetness. Beets are packed with vitamins A and C, beta carotene, potassium, and iron. This smoothie is a powerful cancer fighter, supports a healthy cardiovascular system, and can help treat anemia.

1½ cups peeled and chopped beets
½ cup apple juice
2 cups frozen blueberries
2 cups stemmed kale
2 teaspoons grated peeled fresh ginger
3 ice cubes

In a blender, blend the beets and apple juice until very smooth.

Add the blueberries, kale, ginger, and ice, and blend until thick and smooth.

Serve immediately.

Tip **Peeling beets can create a huge mess and stain your hands, cutting board, clothes, and kitchen, depending on the neatness of your working style. You can wear food-grade kitchen prep gloves to protect your hands. If you do get beet juice on your clothing, treat the stain on both sides as quickly as possible by running it under cold water. Pretreat the stain overnight, and wash as usual.**

Per Serving Calories: 173; Total Fat: 1g; Sodium: 71mg; Protein: 4g

Creamy-Sweet Kale Smoothie

KIDS, GLUTEN-FREES, SINGLETONS, 30-MINUTE

SERVES 2 / PREP: 5 MINUTES / COOK: 0 / TOTAL: 5 MINUTES

Almond butter, the secret ingredient here, adds bulk and a pleasing nutty taste. It is also an excellent source of protein and fiber, as well as being high in vitamin E, magnesium, and iron. You can substitute peanut butter or cashew butter in this tasty smoothie. If you want a vegan version, omit the yogurt or use a soy or coconut product instead.

2 cups stemmed kale
1 cup pineapple chunks
1 cup frozen strawberries
½ cup vanilla Greek yogurt
1 tablespoon almond butter
1 cup water
5 ice cubes

In a blender, combine the kale, pineapple, strawberries, yogurt, almond butter, water, and ice. Blend until smooth.

Enjoy immediately.

Per Serving Calories: 206; Total Fat: 6g; Sodium: 50mg; Protein: 9g

Minted Kale Smoothie

VEGANS, PALEOS, GLUTEN-FREES, SINGLETONS, 30-MINUTE

SERVES 2 / PREP: 10 MINUTES / COOK: 0 / TOTAL: 10 MINUTES

A little bit of mint goes a long way in smoothies, and the amount in this recipe creates an assertive, cool mint flavor. The coolness of this popular herb comes from a component called menthol. Mint is high in vitamins A and C, which can boost immunity, cleanse the blood, and promote healthy digestion, including reducing nausea.

2 cups frozen blueberries
1 cup stemmed kale
¼ cup fresh mint leaves
2 tablespoons almond butter
4 Medjool dates, pitted
4 ice cubes

In a blender, blend the blueberries, kale, mint, almond butter, dates, and ice until smooth.

Serve immediately.

Tip Whenever possible, use Medjool dates in recipes because they are the sweetest variety. Most specialty markets carry this type of date, although any smaller type of date will be fine in a pinch. If you cannot find any dates in your local stores, date paste is a simple alternative.

Per Serving Calories: 253; Total Fat: 10g; Sodium: 19mg; Protein: 6g

Cranberry-Citrus-Kale Smoothie

VEGANS, PALEOS, GLUTEN-FREES, SINGLETONS, 30-MINUTE

SERVES 2 / PREP: 5 MINUTES / COOK: 0 / TOTAL: 5 MINUTES

If you're a fan of tart tastes, this is the smoothie for you. The cranberry, lemon, and kale will get your eyes open and put a little extra spring in your step. A few tablespoons of mint, lemongrass, or thyme would add to the fresh flavor of this drink. The intense citrus-cranberry taste can also make lovely frozen treats or sorbet if you want a unique dessert.

4 cups stemmed kale
2 cups unsweetened cranberry juice
2 cups frozen banana chunks
2 oranges, peeled and cut into chunks
1 tablespoon orange zest
1 tablespoon freshly squeezed lemon juice

In a blender, blend the kale, cranberry juice, bananas, oranges, orange zest, and lemon juice until smooth.

Serve immediately.

Tip **Use pure unsweetened cranberry juice rather than sweetened juice cocktail, or you will be adding more sugar to your smoothie than you might want. You can also throw in a few fresh cranberries if you are a die-hard fan of this tart berry.**

Per Serving Calories: 342; Total Fat: 1g; Sodium: 96mg; Protein: 7g

Creamy Green Kale Smoothie

VEGANS, PALEOS, GLUTEN-FREES, SINGLETONS, 30-MINUTE

SERVES 2 / PREP: 5 MINUTES / COOK: 0 / TOTAL: 5 MINUTES

Avocado creates a luscious velvety texture in this smoothie. You might even think someone added ice cream! Avocado is an excellent source of monounsaturated fats and provides fiber, oleic acid, omega-3 fatty acids, and lutein. Adding an avocado to kale smoothies and juices is even more beneficial because half an avocado can increase the body's absorption of the fat-soluble beta carotene in kale by as much as 400 percent.

2 cups stemmed kale
1 cup spinach leaves
1 cup apple juice
2 cups frozen banana chunks
½ avocado

In a blender, blend the kale, spinach, apple juice, bananas, and avocado until smooth.

Serve immediately.

Tip Avocados ripen well at home in paper bags, if you can't find a ready-to-eat one in the store. For a superior flavor, look for avocados with short necks rather than rounded tops because this means the fruit was ripened on the tree. They should also have no sunken spots or cracks in the skin.

Per Serving Calories: 302; Total Fat: 10g; Sodium: 49mg; Protein: 5g

Herbed Raspberry-Kale Smoothie

VEGANS, PALEOS, GLUTEN-FREES, SINGLETONS, 30-MINUTE

SERVES 2 / PREP: 5 MINUTES / COOK: 0 / TOTAL: 5 MINUTES

Herbs are an often-overlooked addition to smoothies, which is unfortunate because these fresh ingredients add depth of flavor and many health benefits. If you don't have parsley or mint, then thyme, basil, savory, lemon balm, or oregano would all be lovely in this recipe. Fresh raspberries can be substituted for the frozen ones in equal amounts.

3 cups stemmed kale
1 frozen banana
1 cup frozen raspberries
½ cup apple juice
¼ cup chopped parsley
1 tablespoon chopped fresh mint

In a blender, blend the kale, banana, raspberries, apple juice, parsley, and mint until very smooth.

Serve immediately.

Per Serving Calories: 264; Total Fat: 1g; Sodium: 52mg; Protein: 5g

Fennel–Kale Smoothie

VEGANS, PALEOS, GLUTEN-FREES, SINGLETONS, 30-MINUTE

SERVES 2 / PREP: 10 MINUTES / COOK: 0 / TOTAL: 10 MINUTES

This smoothie contains many different ingredients and flavors that work well together and provide lots of energy for your day. Figs are high in natural sugar but can have a laxative effect, so don't throw any extra into this drink. The subtle licorice taste of the fennel complements the figs beautifully and provides lots of bulk to support a healthy digestive system.

3 cups stemmed kale
1 cup chopped fennel
1 cup chopped fresh figs
2 tablespoons almond butter
½ cup freshly squeezed orange juice
1 teaspoon orange zest
½ cup water
4 ice cubes

In a blender, blend the kale, fennel, figs, almond butter, orange juice, orange zest, water, and ice cubes until smooth.

Serve immediately.

Tip Fennel is an undeniably elegant vegetable with a gently curving bulb topped by ethereal, feathery fronds. These fronds make a lovely garnish on your smoothie or fish dishes. This fibrous ingredient is in season in the early spring and late fall.

Per Serving Calories: 216; Total Fat: 9g; Sodium: 67mg; Protein: 8g

Ginger–Almond–Kale Smoothie

KIDS, VEGANS, PALEOS, GLUTEN-FREES, SINGLETONS, 30-MINUTE

SERVES 2 / PREP: 5 MINUTES / COOK: 0 / TOTAL: 5 MINUTES

Fresh ginger is very different from ground ginger. If you typically use ground ginger in your cooking, the amount of fresh ginger here may be a shock. One teaspoon of fresh ginger is the equivalent of ⅛ teaspoon of ground ginger, and has a milder flavor due to its moisture content. For a stronger flavor, simply add more ginger. You'll be doing your body a favor, as ginger is wonderful for easing digestion and boosts the immune system, too.

2 cups stemmed kale
1 cup almond milk
1 cup frozen banana chunks
1 cup frozen peach slices
1 tablespoon grated peeled fresh ginger
Pinch ground cinnamon

In a blender, blend the kale, almond milk, banana, peaches, ginger, and cinnamon until smooth.

Serve immediately.

Tip Almond milk used to be difficult to find in mainstream grocery stores. While easier to find now, this creamy, almost flowery-tasting milk is actually very easy to make at home. Just put about 3 cups of filtered water in a blender, add 1 cup of raw almonds, and blend until the water looks milky and the almonds are finely chopped. Strain the liquid through a cheesecloth into a container, and squeeze the solids in the cloth to get every sweet drop of the milk. Refrigerate the milk for up to two weeks.

Per Serving Calories: 148; Total Fat: 2g; Sodium: 120mg; Protein: 4g

Fresh Minty Mango-Kale Smoothie

KIDS, VEGANS, PALEOS, GLUTEN-FREES, SINGLETONS, 30-MINUTE

SERVES 2 / PREP: 5 MINUTES / COOK: 0 / TOTAL: 5 MINUTES

Mangoes have a lovely, piney taste and add brilliant color to smoothies. The strong taste of this sunny fruit offsets the hefty amount of kale here to create a sweetish smoothie with a creamy finish. If you want to substitute fresh mango for frozen, opt for ripe mangoes that give when you press them with your fingertips. The riper the fruit, the sweeter the result.

3 cups stemmed kale
1 cup vanilla almond milk
½ English cucumber, cut into chunks
1 cup frozen mango pieces
2 tablespoons freshly squeezed lemon juice
2 tablespoons chopped fresh mint
1 teaspoon lemon zest

In a blender, blend the kale, vanilla almond milk, cucumber, mango, lemon juice, mint, and lemon zest until smooth.

Serve immediately.

Per Serving Calories: 129; Total Fat: 2g; Sodium: 130mg; Protein: 5g

Pastel Melon–Kale Smoothie

VEGANS, PALEOS, GLUTEN-FREES, SINGLETONS, 30-MINUTE

SERVES 2 / PREP: 10 MINUTES / COOK: 0 / TOTAL: 10 MINUTES

This recipe makes a very green smoothie. Every ingredient other than the apple juice is either pale or dark green. When you put the green grapes in the freezer for this recipe, you might want to freeze extras because frozen grapes are a fabulously healthy treat. Grapes are not a common smoothie ingredient, but adding them will help lower your risk of heart disease and reduce the risk of blood clots, as grapes are high in the antioxidant resveratrol. Grapes are also an excellent source of vitamins A, C, E, and K as well as manganese.

3 cups stemmed kale
2 cups frozen green seedless grapes
2 cups honeydew melon pieces
4 celery stalks
½ cup apple juice

In a blender, blend the kale, grapes, honeydew melon, celery, and apple juice until smooth.

Serve immediately.

Per Serving Calories: 261; Total Fat: 0g; Sodium: 107mg; Protein: 4g

Rosy Kale Juice

SERVES 2 / PREP: 10 MINUTES / COOK: 0 / TOTAL: 10 MINUTES

Kale leaves can sometimes be difficult to push through a juicer, especially if the kale is a little older and not so tender. Put the kale through first, and use the other vegetables to force the leaves into the blades. The red cabbage in this recipe juices very well, but can be slightly bitter. It can also cause gas if you aren't used to eating it, so feel free to reduce the amount in that case. Cabbage can help lower cholesterol, fight cancer, and improve the symptoms of arthritis.

3½ cups stemmed kale
½ head red cabbage, quartered
2 beets, halved
3 celery stalks
1 pear, halved and cored

In a juicer, process the kale and cabbage, pushing the leaves through with the beet pieces and celery stalks, then juice the pear.

Serve immediately.

Per Serving Calories: 196; Total Fat: 3g; Sodium: 252mg; Protein: 15g

Piña Colada–Kale Smoothie

KIDS, VEGANS, PALEOS, GLUTEN-FREES, SINGLETONS, 30-MINUTE

SERVES 2 / PREP: 10 MINUTES / COOK: 0 / TOTAL: 10 MINUTES

Coconut and pineapple are often combined to create a tropical theme. The lime juice brightens the flavor in this smoothie and adds a boost of vitamin C. When you make this recipe, leave some white pith on the lime because it contains a phytochemical called limonene. In an article by Jessica A. Miller and colleagues in *Cancer Prevention Research,* limonene is shown to induce a signal in the body, called apoptosis, which can kill cancer cells and prevent them from dividing at all.

3 cups stemmed kale

1½ cups pineapple chunks

1 cup coconut milk

½ lime, peeled

1 tablespoon hemp seeds

3 ice cubes

In a blender, blend the kale, pineapple, coconut milk, lime, hemp seeds, and ice cubes until smooth.

Serve immediately.

Tip You can make your own coconut milk if you have a blender, cheesecloth, and a little time. In a blender, blend 4 cups of water and 1 cup unsweetened shredded coconut for about 5 minutes, or until the water looks very milky. Pour the mixture through a fine cheesecloth over a bowl, squeezing out every bit of liquid from the cloth that you can. Refrigerate the milk for up to one week. Save the solids left in the cheesecloth to use as coconut flour in another recipe.

Per Serving Calories: 160; Total Fat: 4g; Sodium: 53mg; Protein: 5g

Berry-Kale Juice

KIDS, VEGANS, PALEOS, GLUTEN-FREES, SINGLETONS, 30-MINUTE

SERVES 2 / PREP: 10 MINUTES / COOK: 0 / TOTAL: 10 MINUTES

Many juices feature carrots because they have a pleasing sweet taste as well as many health benefits and are inexpensive. Carrots are high in vitamins A, C, E, and K. Juicing these vibrant root vegetables makes the nutrients more available to the body and allows them to be absorbed more easily. You can juice carrots without peeling them, as long as you scrub them well to remove any pesticide residue.

3½ cups stemmed kale
6 carrots
1 pint fresh strawberries
2 red delicious apples, cored
Pinch ground cinnamon

In a juicer, juice the kale, pushing it through with the carrots.

Juice the strawberries and apples, and stir together with the kale-carrot juice.

Stir in a pinch of cinnamon, and serve immediately.

Tip For a truly intense-flavored juice, make this recipe when strawberries are in season. Pick a pint yourself right from the field. Ripe strawberries are so luscious, you might catch the fragrance of the berries on the breeze long before you reach the field.

Per Serving Calories: 287; Total Fat: 4g; Sodium: 252mg; Protein: 15g

Lemony Green Juice

SERVES 2 / PREP: 10 MINUTES / COOK: 0 / TOTAL: 10 MINUTES

This smoothie is tart, vibrantly green, and brimming with healthy nutrients and energy-boosting antioxidants. The apples provide some sweetness. If you don't need a vegan version, you can stir in a little honey when the juice is done. Most people don't juice apples with the cores because apple seeds contain cyanide. The amount of cyanide is very low, though, so if you happen to juice a few seeds, don't panic.

3½ cups stemmed kale
3½ cups spinach
2 green apples, cored and cut into chunks
1 English cucumber, cut into chunks
½ lemon, peel on

In a juicer, juice the kale and spinach, pushing the leaves through with the apple pieces and cucumber.

Juice the lemon, and stir.

Serve immediately.

Per Serving Calories: 268; Total Fat: 5g; Sodium: 378mg; Protein: 25g

Kiwi-Kale Juice

VEGANS, PALEOS, GLUTEN-FREES, SINGLETONS, 30-MINUTE

SERVES 2 / PREP: 10 MINUTES / COOK: 0 / TOTAL: 10 MINUTES

Kiwi comes in both green and golden varieties, and either can be used in this recipe. Use ripe kiwis, as unripe kiwis are extremely tart. Hold the kiwi gently in a cupped hand, and press lightly with your fingertips to determine the ripeness of the fruit. The skin should give under the pressure. Kiwi contains chlorophyll, which can help detoxify the body and protect against cancer and respiratory disease.

3½ cups stemmed kale
4 kiwis, peeled and cut into chunks
1-inch piece peeled fresh ginger
2 pears, cored and cut into chunks
3 celery stalks, cut into chunks

In a juicer, juice the kale, kiwis, and ginger, pushing the ingredients through with the pear pieces and celery.

Serve immediately.

Tip Fresh ginger can keep in the refrigerator for several weeks as long as it is in a sealed bag. Check it regularly for mold and shriveling. You can also freeze pieces of ginger for up to one month. It can still get moldy in the freezer, so look carefully before using it in your juice.

Juice the ginger early in the process so the rest of the ingredients wash the ginger juice out of the juicer.

Per Serving Calories: 249; Total Fat: 4g; Sodium: 170mg; Protein: 14g

Zesty Cherry Tomato-Kale Juice

VEGANS, PALEOS, GLUTEN-FREES, SINGLETONS, 30-MINUTE

SERVES 2 / PREP: 10 MINUTES / COOK: 0 / TOTAL: 10 MINUTES

Fruits and vegetables are often used together in juices to create a pleasing balance between tart and sweet tastes. This smoothie is not sweet due to the addition of horseradish. You can omit this hot ingredient if it doesn't appeal to your palate. Horseradish is best, and hottest, when freshly grated. Simply juice a 2-inch piece of this pungent root wrapped in a kale leaf.

3½ cups stemmed kale
2 pints cherry tomatoes
1 lemon, peeled
6 celery stalks
1 teaspoon prepared horseradish
Pinch freshly ground black pepper

In a juicer, juice the kale, cherry tomatoes, and lemon, pushing the ingredients through with the celery.

Stir in the horseradish, or juice fresh horseradish if desired.

Season with pepper, and serve plain or over ice.

Per Serving Calories: 155; Total Fat: 4g; Sodium: 217mg; Protein: 16g

4

Breakfasts

Egg White & Kale Scramble

PALEOS, GLUTEN-FREES, SINGLETONS, 30-MINUTE

SERVES 2 / PREP: 10 MINUTES / COOK: 15 MINUTES / TOTAL: 25 MINUTES

This simple, protein-packed breakfast will start your day off right. You can eat this festive scramble on a plate with a little fresh fruit, or tuck it into a tortilla for a grab-and-go wrap. This is also a perfect breakfast-for-dinner dish because it can be thrown together quickly at the end of the day—and is filling enough to satisfy you until breakfast the next day.

Cooking spray
2 cups stemmed and shredded baby kale
1 tomato, seeded and chopped
½ yellow bell pepper, seeded and chopped
Sea salt
Freshly ground black pepper
½ sweet onion, chopped
1 teaspoon minced garlic
8 egg whites
2 teaspoons chopped fresh parsley

Coat a small skillet over medium heat with cooking spray.

Add the kale, tomato, and bell pepper, and sauté for about 6 minutes, or until softened.

Season the kale mixture with sea salt and pepper. Remove from the heat and set aside.

Liberally spray a large skillet over medium-high heat with cooking spray.

Add the onion and garlic, and sauté for about 4 minutes, or until translucent.

Add the egg whites to the skillet, and cook, scrambling, for about 3 minutes, or until dry.

Add the kale mixture to the scrambled egg whites, and stir until well combined.

Top with parsley and serve.

Tip Seeding a tomato is an easy process that starts with cutting it into quarters. Then press the flat of your knife at one end of the tomato and gently cut out the seeds, leaving the outer shell intact.

Per Serving Calories: 124; Total Fat: 1g; Sodium: 370mg; Protein: 17g

Baked Kale Egg Cups

GLUTEN-FREES, SINGLETONS

SERVES 4 / PREP: 10 MINUTES / COOK: 35 MINUTES / TOTAL: 45 MINUTES

If you like to entertain for brunch, this is an elegant recipe to make for your guests. The egg yolks are runny, and the whites cook up tender on their bed of wilted kale. You can put this entire recipe together the night before and refrigerate the ramekins in the baking dish until you are ready to pop them into the oven. Simply eliminate the Parmesan cheese and use grass-fed butter for a Paleo version of the dish.

Cooking spray
1 tablespoon butter
1 sweet onion, thinly sliced
1 teaspoon minced garlic
4 cups stemmed and chopped baby kale
8 large eggs
Sea salt
Freshly ground black pepper
¼ cup grated Parmesan cheese, divided
Hot water, for baking

Preheat the oven to 375°F.

Lightly coat 4 (6-ounce) ramekins with cooking spray. Place them in a baking dish large enough to hold all 4 ramekins and set aside.

In a large skillet over medium-high heat, melt the butter. Add the onion and garlic, and sauté for about 6 minutes, or until lightly caramelized.

Add the kale to the skillet, tossing with tongs until it is wilted but still slightly crisp, about 4 minutes.

Evenly divide the kale among the ramekins.

Crack 2 eggs into each ramekin, and season lightly with sea salt and pepper.

Sprinkle 1 tablespoon of Parmesan over the eggs in each ramekin.

Place the baking dish into the preheated oven. Carefully pour hot water into the dish until it rises to about 1 inch on the sides of the ramekins.

Bake for about 25 minutes, or until the eggs are set, and serve.

Per Serving Calories: 238; Total Fat: 15g; Sodium: 363mg; Protein: 18g

Kale Eggs Florentine

SINGLETONS, MAKE AHEAD, ONE POT

SERVES 4 / PREP: 10 MINUTES / COOK: 25 MINUTES / TOTAL: 35 MINUTES

Eggs have endured an undeserved reputation for decades as an unhealthy food, especially egg yolks. This idea has been debunked, and eggs are back in the good graces of nutritionists everywhere. Eggs contain many important nutrients, as well as nine amino acids and the antioxidants lutein and zeaxanthin. This means eggs are fabulous for the eyes and can help prevent cataracts from forming.

1 teaspoon extra-virgin olive oil
1 sweet onion, chopped
2 teaspoons minced garlic
4 teaspoons all-purpose flour
2 cups 2-percent milk
1 tablespoon Dijon mustard
Sea salt
Freshly ground black pepper
3 cups tightly packed stemmed and
    chopped kale
8 eggs

In a large skillet over medium heat, heat the olive oil. Add the onion and garlic, and sauté for about 4 minutes, or until tender.

Stir in the flour, and cook for 2 minutes. Gradually whisk in the milk. Cook, whisking constantly, for about 4 minutes, until the sauce boils and thickens.

Whisk in the mustard, and season with sea salt and pepper.

Stir in the kale, and cook for about 5 minutes, or until the kale is wilted. Reduce the heat enough that the mixture simmers.

Using the back of a spoon, make 8 deep wells in the kale mixture. Crack 1 egg into each well.

Cover the skillet, and cook for about 6 minutes, until the egg whites are set, but the yolks still runny.

Serve 2 eggs per person with equal amounts of the kale mixture.

Tip The sauce used here is essentially a béchamel, which uses milk and a cooked flour base. You can also try a velouté sauce for extra flavor by simply swapping the milk for chicken broth.

Per Serving Calories: 265; Total Fat: 14g; Sodium: 322mg; Protein: 19g

Decadent Egg Sandwiches

KIDS, SINGLETONS, 30-MINUTE

SERVES 2 / PREP: 10 MINUTES / COOK: 10 MINUTES / TOTAL: 20 MINUTES

The sheer volume and rich taste of this sandwich will make it a favorite choice for lazy mornings after a festive night, or make it a special breakfast for two when you want to impress your partner. The slight saltiness of the sun-dried tomato, the assertive kale, and the creamy avocado will tease your palate—if you can get the whole sandwich in your mouth for a big bite.

2 teaspoons extra-virgin olive oil
2 cups stemmed and chopped kale
4 oil-packed sun-dried tomatoes, coarsely chopped
2 artichoke hearts, coarsely chopped
2 eggs
Sea salt
Freshly ground black pepper
2 thick slices Cheddar cheese
2 crusty buns
½ avocado, sliced

In a medium skillet over medium-high heat, heat the olive oil. Add the kale, and sauté for about 4 minutes, or until wilted. Add the sun-dried tomatoes and artichoke hearts, and sauté for 2 minutes more.

Move the kale mixture to one side of the skillet, and crack the eggs into the empty side.

Fry the eggs for about 3 minutes, or until they are set but the yolks are still runny.

Remove the skillet from the heat, and season the eggs lightly with sea salt and pepper.

Place 1 slice of cheese on the bottom half of each bun. Top each cheese slice with 1 egg.

Top each egg with half of the kale mixture, and arrange half of the avocado slices over each sandwich.

Top each sandwich with the remaining bun halves, and serve.

Tip The leftover avocado half can be used in smoothies, dips, and baking, and on salads. Refrigerate it, tightly wrapped in plastic, for up to three days.

Per Serving Calories: 577; Total Fat: 27g; Sodium: 863mg; Protein: 30g

Kale & Egg White Omelet

GLUTEN-FREES, SINGLETONS, 30-MINUTE

SERVES 2 / PREP: 10 MINUTES / COOK: 10 MINUTES / TOTAL: 20 MINUTES

Scallions might just seem like an accent or garnish in some recipes, but this slender, elegant ingredient also adds a tasty boost to this dish. Scallions are very nutritious and a fabulous source of many vitamins, such as A, B, C, and K. Look for pencil-thin scallions because the taste is better. For an almost sweet flavor, look for snowy bulbs and tender yet firm green stalks on these immature lily plants.

2 tablespoons extra-virgin olive oil
1½ cups stemmed and finely shredded kale
2 scallions, chopped
Sea salt
Freshly ground black pepper
8 egg whites
1 tablespoon water
2 tablespoons chickpea flour
Cooking spray

In a medium skillet over medium-high heat, heat the olive oil.

Add the kale and scallions, and sauté for about 5 minutes, or until the kale is wilted. Season the mixture with sea salt and pepper, and remove the skillet from the heat.

In a large bowl, whisk the egg whites with the water for about 3 minutes, or until frothy. Then whisk in the chickpea flour until smooth.

Liberally coat a large skillet over medium heat with cooking spray. Add the egg whites. Swirl the pan and lift the edges of the cooked egg to allow the uncooked egg to run underneath until the eggs are just set, about 2 minutes.

Spoon the kale mixture over one half of the cooked eggs, and fold the other half of the eggs over the kale. Cut the omelet in half, and serve one half per person.

Tip **If your skillet has a nonstick coating, do not use cooking spray. The coating on the skillet can react with the spray, creating an unhealthy residue.**

Per Serving Calories: 282; Total Fat: 16g; Sodium: 368mg; Protein: 19g

Kale-Bacon Quiche

KIDS, MEAT LOVERS, LARGE GROUPS, MAKE AHEAD

SERVES 8 / PREP: 20 MINUTES / COOK: 55 MINUTES / TOTAL: 1 HOUR, 15 MINUTES

This is a kitchen-sink-style quiche—absolutely crammed with hearty ingredients. The premade crust used here can be replaced with your favorite recipe if you don't mind the extra time and work. Whatever crust you use needs to be deep enough to hold everything. For a different taste, you can use a smoked Gouda or Gruyère cheese instead of the Cheddar.

1 (9-inch) prepared deep-dish pie shell
1 teaspoon extra-virgin olive oil
½ sweet onion, finely diced
½ red bell pepper, diced
3 cups shredded and stemmed kale
½ cup chopped cooked bacon
½ cup shredded sharp Cheddar cheese
4 eggs
½ cup milk
½ cup heavy cream
½ teaspoon ground nutmeg
Sea salt
Freshly ground black pepper

Preheat the oven to 400°F. Line the pie shell with foil, and fill it with dried beans or pie weights.

Bake the shell in the preheated oven for about 12 minutes, or until the rim is light brown.

Remove the shell from the oven, take out the foil and the beans, and set aside to cool. Reduce the oven to 350°F.

In a large skillet over medium-high heat, heat the olive oil. Add the onion and red bell pepper, and sauté for about 4 minutes, or until the vegetables are softened. Add the kale, and toss until wilted, about 6 minutes.

Remove the skillet from the heat. Spoon the vegetable mixture into the pie shell, and top with the bacon and Cheddar.

In a medium bowl, whisk together the eggs, milk, heavy cream, nutmeg, sea salt, and pepper.

Pour the egg mixture into the pie shell.

Carefully place the filled shell in the preheated oven. Bake the quiche for 30 minutes, or until a knife inserted in the center comes out clean. Serve warm.

Per Serving Calories: 152; Total Fat: 11g; Sodium: 320mg; Protein: 8g

Kale—Peameal Frittata

KIDS, MEAT LOVERS, GLUTEN-FREES, LARGE GROUPS, SINGLETONS, ONE POT, MAKE AHEAD

SERVES 4 / PREP: 10 MINUTES / COOK: 30 MINUTES / TOTAL: 40 MINUTES

Frittatas are sometimes confused with omelets because some of the same ingredients are used, and these dishes can look similar. A frittata is assembled completely in a large skillet, with all the ingredients stirred into the eggs. It's then set on the stove to cook, and finished in the oven under the broiler. Omelets are usually beaten eggs cooked to a fluffy finish on the stovetop and then folded over delicious ingredients.

Cooking spray
6 eggs
½ cup sour cream
1 tablespoon chopped fresh basil
Pinch sea salt
Pinch freshly ground black pepper
2½ cups stemmed and finely chopped kale
1 cup diced cooked peameal bacon or regular bacon
1 cup diced cooked sweet potato
½ red bell pepper, finely diced
1 scallion, chopped

Preheat the oven to 350°F.

Lightly coat a deep 10-by-10-inch baking dish with cooking spray and set aside.

In a large bowl, whisk together the eggs, sour cream, basil, sea salt, and pepper.

Stir in the kale, peameal bacon, sweet potato, red bell pepper, and scallion.

Pour the mixture into the prepared baking dish.

Put the dish in the preheated oven, and bake for about 30 minutes, or until a knife inserted in the center comes out clean.

Serve.

Tip **Peameal bacon, also known as Canadian bacon, is characterized by** a cornmeal coating. This bacon is more like ham than standard bacon. It's actually a boneless pork loin that is pickled, meaning it's low in fat and doesn't crisp when fried.

Per Serving Calories: 341; Total Fat: 17g; Sodium: 926mg; Protein: 26g

Pumpkin & Kale Frittata

KIDS, GLUTEN-FREES, LARGE GROUPS, SINGLETONS, ONE POT, MAKE AHEAD

SERVES 4 / PREP: 10 MINUTES / COOK: 35 MINUTES / TOTAL: 45 MINUTES

Don't be surprised to see intact chunks of feta cheese when you take this pretty dish out of the oven. Feta cheese does not melt like other cheeses. This unprocessed sheep's milk cheese is much higher in vitamin D than cow's milk cheeses and has fewer calories. If you're worried about sodium in your diet, look for low-sodium feta the next time you go shopping.

1 tablespoon extra-virgin olive oil
4 cups diced pumpkin or butternut squash
2 teaspoons minced garlic
½ teaspoon ground cumin
½ teaspoon ground coriander
¼ teaspoon ground nutmeg
3 cups stemmed and chopped kale
8 eggs, beaten
¼ cup whole milk
1 scallion, chopped
Sea salt
Freshly ground black pepper
½ cup crumbled feta cheese

Preheat the oven to 425°F. In a large ovenproof skillet over medium-high heat, heat the olive oil.

Add the pumpkin, and sauté for about 5 minutes, or until cooked through and lightly browned.

Add the garlic, cumin, coriander, and nutmeg, and sauté for 2 minutes more.

Add the kale and cook, tossing with tongs, for about 4 minutes, or until wilted. Remove the skillet from the heat.

In a large bowl, whisk together the eggs, milk, scallion, sea salt, and pepper. Sprinkle the eggs with the feta, and pour the mixture into the skillet.

Put the skillet in the preheated oven, and bake for about 15 minutes, or until the frittata sets and is lightly browned.

Remove the skillet from the oven and let stand for 5 minutes. Serve one-quarter frittata per person.

Tip **Make sure the feta you buy is made with sheep's milk, not cow's milk. Cow's milk feta crumbles very easily and won't give you those nice salty pockets in the finished dish.**

Per Serving Calories: 345; Total Fat: 19g; Sodium: 449mg; Protein: 20g

Egg-Kale Tacos

KIDS, SINGLETONS, 30-MINUTE

SERVES 4 / PREP: 15 MINUTES / COOK: 5 MINUTES / TOTAL: 20 MINUTES

Corn taco shells are often used only for meals eaten later in the day. That's a pity, because they taste lovely with eggs for breakfast. Warming the tacos ensures they'll hold together rather than shatter while you eat your taco. You can also put taco shells in the microwave for 30 seconds to make them more flexible.

4 corn taco shells
1 teaspoon extra-virgin olive oil
6 eggs, beaten
4 cups shredded Blanched Kale (page 33)
Sea salt
Freshly ground black pepper
1 tomato, finely chopped
1 cup shredded Cheddar cheese, divided
4 teaspoons chopped jalapeño peppers, divided

Preheat the oven to 250°F.

Wrap the taco shells in a clean kitchen towel, and put them in the oven.

In a small skillet over medium-high heat, heat the olive oil.

Add the eggs to the skillet, and cook, scrambling, for about 4 minutes, or until they are fluffy, cooked through, and dry.

Stir in the Blanched Kale, and remove the skillet from the heat.

Season the mixture with sea salt and pepper.

Remove the taco shells from the oven, and evenly divide the egg mixture among the warmed shells.

Top each taco with ¼ of the chopped tomato, ¼ cup of Cheddar, and 1 teaspoon of jalapeño peppers.

Serve immediately.

Per Serving Calories: 229; Total Fat: 12g; Sodium: 197mg; Protein: 13g

Kale, Steak & Mushroom Breakfast Skillet

KIDS, MEAT LOVERS, PALEOS, GLUTEN-FREES, LARGE GROUPS, SINGLETONS, MAKE AHEAD

SERVES 4 / PREP: 10 MINUTES / COOK: 30 MINUTES / TOTAL: 40 MINUTES

Mushrooms have a rich, earthy flavor that combines beautifully with kale and creamy goat cheese. You can use an assortment of mushrooms in this casserole, such as shiitake, oyster, enoki, and even meaty portobello. If you want to use portobello mushrooms, scoop out and discard the black gills before chopping. The gills can turn the egg mixture a dingy gray.

2 tablespoons extra-virgin olive oil

1 pound sirloin steak, trimmed and cut into ½-inch chunks

2 cups sliced mushrooms

4 cups finely chopped kale, stemmed, thoroughly washed, and patted dry

1 leek, washed and finely chopped

Sea salt

Freshly ground black pepper

4 large eggs

Chili powder, for garnish

Preheat the oven to 375°F. In a large ovenproof skillet over medium-high heat, heat the olive oil.

Add the steak, and sauté, stirring occasionally, until the meat is browned and almost cooked through, about 6 minutes.

Add the mushrooms, and sauté for about 5 minutes, or until they are lightly browned. Add the kale and leek, and sauté for about 5 minutes more, until the kale is wilted. Season the mixture with sea salt and pepper.

Using the back of a spoon, make 4 wells in the kale mixture, and carefully crack an egg into each well.

Put the skillet in the preheated oven, and bake until the egg whites are set, about 10 minutes. Garnish with chili powder, and serve.

Tip The lovely layers in leeks can be filled with gritty dirt, so wash these vegetables carefully. Slice the leeks, and swish them around in a bowl full of water. Let the dirt settle to the bottom of the bowl, and scoop out the leeks.

Per Serving Calories: 394; Total Fat: 19g; Sodium: 180mg; Protein: 44g

Kale Breakfast Burritos

KIDS, MEAT LOVERS, SINGLETONS, 30-MINUTE

SERVES 4 / PREP: 10 MINUTES / COOK: 20 MINUTES / TOTAL: 30 MINUTES

Sausage and kale are a natural pairing, especially if the kale is sautéed in the rendered sausage fat along with the cooked potatoes. If you plan to eat these burritos on the run, dice the potatoes small enough that they'll wrap easily in the tortillas. You can assemble them completely and simply microwave the burrito for one minute when you want a snack or quick breakfast.

Cooking spray
8 ounces sausage meat
2 cooked Yukon gold potatoes, cut into
    ¼-inch dice
2 scallions, chopped
1 red bell pepper, diced
1 teaspoon minced garlic
½ teaspoon chili powder
Sea salt
Freshly ground black pepper
2 cups stemmed and chopped kale
4 (10-inch) whole-wheat tortillas
4 teaspoons plain Greek yogurt, divided
1 tomato, chopped, divided

Lightly coat a large skillet over medium-high heat with cooking spray. Add the sausage meat, and cook for about 5 minutes, or until lightly browned and no longer pink.

Add the potatoes to the skillet, and sauté until warmed through, about 3 minutes. Stir in the scallions, red bell pepper, and garlic, and sauté for 3 minutes. Stir in the chili powder, and season with sea salt and pepper.

Add the kale to the skillet and cook, tossing with tongs, for about 5 minutes, or until it is wilted. Remove the skillet from the heat.

Lay the tortillas on a clean work surface, and spread 1 teaspoon of yogurt on each. Top each with one-fourth of the chopped tomato.

Evenly divide the sausage-kale mixture among the 4 tortillas, placing it toward the bottom of each.

Working with one tortilla at a time, fold the sides in over the filling. Then fold the bottom up over the filling, and continue rolling the tortilla into a tight cylinder. Serve.

Per Serving Calories: 408; Total Fat: 17g; Sodium: 646mg; Protein: 20g

Colorful Breakfast Wraps

KIDS, SINGLETONS, 30-MINUTE, MAKE AHEAD

SERVES 2 / PREP: 10 MINUTES / COOK: 15 MINUTES / TOTAL: 25 MINUTES

The filling in this dish bursts with festive flecks of red and green from the vegetables and herbs. You can create this omelet, cut it into portions, and freeze them to eat later. Simply remove a portion from the freezer, microwave it for about one minute, and wrap it in a tortilla. There will be no loss of quality or flavor.

1 tablespoon extra-virgin olive oil, divided
1 tomato, chopped
1 scallion, chopped
½ teaspoon minced garlic
4 large kale leaves, stemmed, thoroughly washed, and coarsely chopped
3 eggs
2 tablespoons chopped fresh basil
Pinch crushed red pepper flakes
Pinch sea salt
Freshly ground black pepper
2 (10-inch) whole-wheat tortillas

In a medium skillet over medium-high heat, heat 1½ teaspoons of olive oil.

Add the tomato, scallion, and garlic, and sauté for about 3 minutes, or until softened.

Add the kale to the skillet, and sauté for about 3 minutes, stirring, until the kale wilts but is still bright green. Remove from the heat and set aside.

In a small skillet over medium-high heat, heat the remaining 1½ teaspoons of olive oil.

In a small bowl, whisk together the eggs, basil, red pepper flakes, sea salt, and pepper.

Pour the eggs into the skillet, swirling for about 2 minutes, or until they start to set.

Lift the edges of the egg mixture to allow the uncooked egg to flow underneath. Continue to swirl and lift the eggs for another 3 to 4 minutes, or until they are just cooked through. Remove the skillet from the heat, and cut the omelet in half.

➡

Colorful Breakfast Wraps, continued

Place one omelet half on each tortilla, near the bottom, and top each with equal amounts of the kale mixture.

Working with one tortilla at a time, fold the sides in and over the filling. Then fold the bottom up over the filling, and continue rolling the tortilla into a tight wrap.

Tip For a different flavor, try varying the herbs you use. Replace the basil with dill or cilantro, depending on your preference.

Per Serving Calories: 319; Total Fat: 15g; Sodium: 311mg; Protein: 17g

Kale Breakfast Cassoulet

VEGANS, GLUTEN-FREES, LARGE GROUPS, SINGLETONS, 30-MINUTE, ONE POT, MAKE AHEAD

SERVES 4 / PREP: 10 MINUTES / COOK: 20 MINUTES / TOTAL: 30 MINUTES

How many meals do you prepare that are named after the historical vessel they are cooked in rather than their ingredients or place of origin? The name *cassoulet* comes from *cassole*, which is the earthenware pot in which this rich, slow-cooked stew of beans is traditionally cooked. This French stew usually contains pork or duck, so feel free to include those proteins if you don't want to make this vegan version.

2 teaspoons extra-virgin olive oil
½ sweet onion, chopped
2 teaspoons minced garlic
6 cups stemmed and chopped kale
¾ cup low-sodium vegetable broth
1 tablespoon balsamic vinegar
2 cups cooked black beans
2 cups cooked lentils
1 cup cooked Great Northern beans
1 teaspoon smoked paprika
1 teaspoon sweet paprika
1 teaspoon dried oregano
¼ teaspoon cayenne pepper
Sea salt
Freshly ground black pepper
2 tablespoons chopped fresh basil

In a large saucepan over medium-high heat, heat the olive oil.

Add the onion and garlic, and sauté for about 3 minutes, or until softened.

Add the kale to the pan, and sauté for about 3 more minutes, or until wilted.

Stir in the broth, balsamic vinegar, black beans, lentils, Northern beans, smoked paprika, sweet paprika, oregano, and cayenne pepper.

Bring the mixture to a boil. Reduce the heat to low, and simmer for 10 minutes. Remove from the heat, and season with sea salt and pepper.

Sprinkle with the basil and serve.

Tip Great Northern beans (and their sisters, navy beans and cannelloni beans) can be cooked a long time without losing their shape, so they are good for recipes where you want the integrity of the beans to shine through. These beans also have an almost buttery texture that is brilliant with the kale.

Per Serving Calories: 386; Total Fat: 4g; Sodium: 440mg; Protein: 25g

Kale Breakfast Pizza

KIDS, MEAT LOVERS, SINGLETONS, 30-MINUTE

SERVES 4 / PREP: 10 MINUTES / COOK: 10 MINUTES / TOTAL: 20 MINUTES

If the thought of pizza for breakfast has you envisioning cold leftovers scrounged from a slightly crushed pizza box, you will be pleasantly surprised with this recipe. These are freshly made, nutritious, speedy individual pizzas topped with tasty bacon, crispy kale, and whole, sunny-side-up eggs. Add a splash of your favorite hot sauce and enjoy!

3 cups stemmed and coarsely chopped kale
4 whole pita breads
2 tomatoes, cut into ¼-inch-thick slices
3 bacon slices, cooked and chopped
Pinch red pepper flakes
1 cup shredded mozzarella cheese, divided
4 eggs
Sea salt
Freshly ground black pepper

Preheat the oven to 450°F.

Bring a large stockpot filled with water to a boil on the stove over high heat.

Add the kale and blanch for about 1 minute, or until just wilted.

Drain the kale, squeezing out as much water as possible.

Place the pitas on a baking sheet. Top each pita with an equal amount of tomato slices, kale, and cooked bacon. Add a pinch of red pepper flakes to each pita, then top each with ¼ cup mozzarella cheese.

Using the back of a spoon, make a well in the center of each pizza. Crack 1 egg into each well, and season lightly with sea salt and pepper.

Put the baking sheet in the preheated oven, and bake for about 5 minutes, or until the egg whites are completely set and the cheese is melted and bubbly. Serve.

Tip **Pita breads can be replaced with a single premade pizza crust if you don't need individual pizzas. You can even find gluten-free crusts in most grocery stores.**

Per Serving Calories: 378; Total Fat: 13g; Sodium: 755mg; Protein: 24g

Hearty Kale Breakfast Bowl

KIDS, MEAT LOVERS, GLUTEN-FREES, LARGE GROUPS, 30-MINUTE, ONE POT

SERVES 4 / PREP: 10 MINUTES / COOK: 15 MINUTES / TOTAL: 25 MINUTES

Breakfast bowls are just tasty ingredients mixed together, rather than laid out on a plate in a traditional presentation. This stew and casserole all in one is filling, and a great choice for a day where you might be running around without the opportunity to eat. You can top this dish with a fried or poached egg for added energy.

1 tablespoon extra-virgin olive oil
4 cups stemmed and chopped kale
2 teaspoons minced garlic
½ teaspoon red pepper flakes
1 cup cooked quinoa
1 cup cooked lentils
4 cooked bacon slices, chopped
1 pint cherry tomatoes, halved
4 scallions, thinly sliced
½ cup grated Parmesan cheese

In a large skillet over medium-high heat, heat the olive oil.

Add the kale, and sauté for about 4 minutes, or until it just wilts.

Add the garlic and red pepper flakes, and sauté for 2 minutes more.

Stir in the quinoa, lentils, and bacon, and continue to cook for 6 more minutes.

Add the tomatoes and scallions, tossing together until well mixed.

Top with the Parmesan and serve.

Tip **Quinoa can be quite expensive if you buy it in packages right off the shelf. To save money, look for quinoa in the bulk section of your grocery store, and invest in a few mason jars in which to store this ingredient. Quinoa will keep for over six months if stored in a sealed container in a cool, dry place.**

Per Serving Calories: 293; Total Fat: 11g; Sodium: 312mg; Protein: 17g

Sweet Potato & Kale Skillet

KIDS, PALEOS, GLUTEN-FREES, SINGLETONS, ONE POT

SERVES 4 / PREP: 15 MINUTES / COOK: 30 MINUTES / TOTAL: 45 MINUTES

One-pot meals can be lifesavers, whether you're in a rush in the morning or just have an aversion to cleaning up after cooking. The success of this pretty dish lies in its convenience, simplicity, and deliciousness. That first forkful of rich, oozing egg as it drips through the kale and tender sweet potatoes is absolutely spectacular.

1 tablespoon extra-virgin olive oil
1 sweet onion, chopped
2 sweet potatoes, finely diced
2 parsnips, diced
2 teaspoons minced garlic
4 cups stemmed and chopped kale
8 eggs
Sea salt
Freshly ground black pepper

Preheat the oven to broil.

In a large ovenproof skillet over medium-high heat, heat the olive oil.

Add the onion, and sauté for about 3 minutes, or until softened.

Add the sweet potatoes and parsnips, and sauté for about 15 minutes.

Add the garlic, and sauté for 1 minute more.

Add the kale and sauté, tossing lightly with tongs, for about 5 minutes, or until the kale is wilted.

In a small bowl, crack all 8 eggs and whisk until mixed. Pour egg mixture over kale mixture in the skillet, stirring slightly.

Cook for about 3 minutes.

Remove the skillet from the heat, and place it under the broiler. Broil for about 2 minutes. Remove from the broiler, and season with sea salt and pepper.

Per Serving Calories: 358; Total Fat: 14g; Sodium: 241mg; Protein: 17g

Easy Kale–Potato Hash

PALEOS, GLUTEN-FREES, SINGLETONS

SERVES 4 / PREP: 15 MINUTES / COOK: 45 MINUTES / TOTAL: 1 HOUR

Potatoes are often relegated to the do-not-eat list by people looking to follow a healthier diet. This designation is unfair, as potatoes themselves are not unhealthy. While it's true that some people must avoid potatoes because of their relatively high glycemic index, it's the traditional preparations that sully this versatile tuber's reputation. Potatoes are most often served fried, or mashed with loads of cream and butter, or baked and slathered in cheese, adding unnecessary fat and calories along the way. Potatoes allowed to shine in their natural state are high in fiber, vitamin C, and phytonutrients, while being low in fat. This humble vegetable can help fight certain cancers, promote brain health, and lower blood pressure.

3 medium-size waxy potatoes, peeled
2 tablespoons extra-virgin olive oil, divided
2½ cups stemmed and coarsely chopped kale
1 cup coarsely chopped Swiss chard
½ sweet onion, minced
1 tablespoon horseradish
½ teaspoon minced garlic
½ teaspoon freshly ground black pepper
¼ teaspoon sea salt
2 teaspoons white vinegar
4 eggs

Fill a large pot with water, add the potatoes, and set the pot over high heat. Bring to a boil, and cook for about 20 minutes, or until the potatoes are cooked but still firm.

Drain the potatoes, and set aside to cool.

In a large bowl, shred the cooled potatoes. Set aside.

In a large skillet over medium-high heat, heat 1 teaspoon of olive oil.

Add the kale and chard to the skillet, and sauté for about 5 minutes, or until just wilted.

Transfer the kale mixture to a cutting board, chop finely, and set aside.

Add the onion, horseradish, garlic, pepper, sea salt, and kale to the shredded potatoes, and stir until well mixed.

In a clean, large nonstick skillet over medium heat, heat the remaining 1 tablespoon plus 2 teaspoons of olive oil.

Spread the kale-potato mixture evenly in the hot skillet, and cook for about 20 minutes, stirring frequently, until the potatoes are golden and crispy.

While the potato mixture cooks, begin preparing the eggs. In a 12-inch saucepan over high heat, bring about 3 inches of water to a boil. Add the vinegar, and reduce the heat to medium-low, keeping the water at a simmer.

Crack 1 egg into a small bowl, and pour the egg into the water.

Repeat with the remaining eggs, making sure to pour them in away from each other.

Turn off the heat, and cover the pan. Let the eggs sit for 5 minutes.

Divide the potato hash onto four plates. Using a slotted spoon, carefully transfer 1 poached egg on top of each serving, being sure to let any cooking water drain away first.

Tip This dish is similar to the Swiss dish röesti, except here you are using cooked potatoes instead of raw. It's important to cool the potatoes completely before shredding them, or you'll end up with a mushy mess.

Per Serving Calories: 251; Total Fat: 11g; Sodium: 281mg; Protein: 13g

Pumpkin-Kale Muffins

KIDS, LARGE GROUPS, MAKE AHEAD

MAKES 12 MUFFINS / PREP: 10 MINUTES / COOK: 30 MINUTES / TOTAL: 40 MINUTES

These muffins just might lift your spirits on a groggy morning, as pumpkin contains the amino acid L-tryptophan, which produces feelings of well-being and happiness. Pumpkin is a wonderful base for these colorful muffins—it creates a moist, tender crumb and adds nutritional benefits that complement the kale. You'll need *pure pumpkin* rather than pumpkin pie filling, if using a canned product.

2 cups all-purpose flour
1 teaspoon baking soda
½ teaspoon sea salt
¼ teaspoon ground nutmeg
1½ cups stemmed and finely chopped kale
1 tablespoon chopped fresh basil
3 eggs, lightly beaten
1 cup pumpkin purée
½ cup sour cream
½ cup extra-virgin olive oil

Preheat the oven to 400°F.

Line a 12-muffin pan with paper liners and set aside.

In a large bowl, stir together the flour, baking soda, sea salt, nutmeg, kale, and basil until well combined.

In a medium bowl, whisk together the eggs, pumpkin, sour cream, and olive oil until blended.

Add the wet ingredients to the dry ingredients, stirring until just combined.

Evenly divide the batter among the muffin cups, and bake for about 30 minutes, or until a toothpick inserted in the center comes out clean.

Cool the muffins on a wire rack before serving.

Per Serving (1 muffin) Calories: 198; Total Fat: 12g; Sodium: 210mg; Protein: 5g

Kale Breakfast Stew

KIDS, MEAT LOVERS, PALEOS, GLUTEN-FREES, LARGE GROUPS, SINGLETONS, 30-MINUTE, MAKE AHEAD

SERVES 4 / PREP: 5 MINUTES / COOK: 20 MINUTES / TOTAL: 25 MINUTES

Tomato-infused herb broth studded with thick chunks of ham and heaps of shredded kale form the perfect base for delicate poached eggs. This dish can be considered Paleo as long as the ham is a natural product without added chemicals or preservatives. Ask your favorite butcher for an organic source for ham, bacon, and other meats.

1 teaspoon extra-virgin olive oil
1 sweet onion, thinly sliced
1½ teaspoons minced garlic
4 tomatoes, diced
2 tablespoons tomato paste
¾ cup low-sodium chicken broth
1½ cups diced ham
1 teaspoon chili powder
4 cups stemmed and shredded kale
Dash sea salt
Dash freshly ground black pepper
3 cups water
2 teaspoons white vinegar
4 eggs

In a large skillet over medium-high heat, heat the olive oil.

Add the onions and garlic, and sauté for about 4 minutes, or until the onions are translucent.

Stir in the tomatoes, tomato paste, chicken broth, ham, and chili powder. Bring the mixture to a boil. Reduce the heat to low, and simmer for 4 minutes.

Add the kale to the skillet, and season with sea salt and pepper. Simmer the mixture for an additional 6 minutes, stirring occasionally.

In a medium saucepan over high heat, boil the water and vinegar. Reduce the heat so the water simmers gently.

Carefully crack 1 egg into a small bowl, and then slip it into the water. Repeat with the remaining 3 eggs. Poach the eggs for about 3 minutes, or until the whites are firm.

Divide the stew into four bowls. Using a slotted spoon, carefully transfer 1 poached egg on top of each serving, being sure to let any cooking water drain completely away first.

Per Serving Calories: 255; Total Fat: 11g; Sodium: 854mg; Protein: 19g

Kale-Cornbread Muffins

KIDS, LARGE GROUPS, 30-MINUTE, MAKE AHEAD

MAKES 12 MUFFINS / PREP: 10 MINUTES / COOK: 20 MINUTES / TOTAL: 30 MINUTES

Cornbread has a long and colorful history, starting with the Native Americans who created this quick bread long before Europeans appeared on the continent's shores. There are many cornbread variations, depending on the region of the country and variety of corn used in the recipe. The Southwest favors blue corn, the North is partial to yellow corn, and Southern states often bake with white corn. All types work well in this recipe.

4 tablespoons (½ stick) melted butter, plus extra for greasing muffin tins
1½ cups buttermilk
¾ cup cornmeal
½ cup corn flour
¼ cup all-purpose flour
1½ teaspoons baking powder
¾ teaspoon baking soda
½ teaspoon sea salt
Pinch ground nutmeg
¾ cup shredded sharp Cheddar cheese
1½ cups stemmed and finely shredded kale

Preheat the oven to 350°F. Generously grease a 12-muffin pan and set aside.

In a small bowl, whisk together the melted butter and buttermilk.

In a large bowl, stir together the cornmeal, corn flour, all-purpose flour, baking powder, baking soda, sea salt, and nutmeg. Add the buttermilk mixture to the dry ingredients, and stir to combine. Fold in the Cheddar and kale.

Equally divide the batter among the muffin cups, and bake for about 20 minutes, or until a toothpick inserted in the center comes out clean.

Remove the muffin tin from the oven and let cool for 5 minutes on a wire rack.

Turn the muffins out onto the rack to cool further, using a knife if necessary to free each muffin from the tin. Serve warm.

Tip Use this recipe as a basic cornbread, and jazz it up with chopped hot peppers, red pepper flakes, bacon, and various cheeses. Cornbread is a great accompaniment to chili or a hearty bowl of soup.

Per Serving (1 muffin) Calories: 205; Total Fat: 15g; Sodium: 330mg; Protein: 5g

5

Snacks

Simple Kale Chips

SERVES 4 / PREP: 10 MINUTES / COOK: 25 MINUTES + 5 MINUTES COOLING / TOTAL: 40 MINUTES

Kale chips are a phenomenon, an obsession, and the subject of countless hours of practice by many in the quest for the perfect crispness. Once you master this basic recipe, you can branch out and add any type of seasoning to create ranch-style, cheese, spicy, or Asian-style chips. You can also use a variety of tasty dips to enhance your perfectly crisped kale chips.

3½ cups kale, stemmed and torn into
    2-inch pieces
1 tablespoon extra-virgin olive oil
¼ teaspoon sea salt

Note You can use aluminum foil in place of the parchment paper. Be aware, though, that parchment does not create the browning level that foil does, so there is a chance the food can burn or become too brown.

Preheat the oven to 300°F.

Line 2 baking sheets with parchment paper and set aside.

Dry the kale completely, either with paper towels or in a salad spinner, and transfer to a large bowl.

Drizzle the kale with the olive oil. Using your hands, toss the kale with the oil to evenly coat each leaf.

Season with sea salt, and toss to coat.

On each baking sheet, spread half the kale in a single layer. If you can't fit it all on the 2 sheets, make another single-layer batch.

Bake for 20 to 25 minutes, rotating half-way through, or until the kale is crispy and dry.

Cool the chips on the sheets for 5 minutes before serving.

Tip It is crucial to dry the kale completely before tossing it in the olive oil or you will have soggy chips instead of perfect crispy leaves. Wet spots will also prevent whatever seasoning you use from adhering evenly.

Per Serving Calories: 58; Total Fat: 4g; Sodium: 142mg; Protein: 2g

Hot Kale-Artichoke Dip

MAKES 3 CUPS / PREP: 10 MINUTES / COOK: 20 MINUTES / TOTAL: 30 MINUTES

A go-to dip is an important dish to have in your culinary repertoire, and this recipe will prove a guaranteed crowd pleaser. Blanching the kale is important to get the right creamy texture, so don't omit this step. The dip can be made ahead to save time, refrigerated, and put in the oven when you need it. Depending on your preference, you can add as much hot sauce as you like to make this dip extra-spicy.

4 ounces cream cheese, at room temperature
½ cup milk
½ cup grated Parmesan cheese
½ cup shredded sharp Cheddar cheese
1 teaspoon minced garlic
¼ teaspoon hot sauce
2 cups chopped Blanched Kale (page 33)
½ cup roughly chopped artichoke hearts

Preheat the oven to 450°F.

In large bowl, stir together the cream cheese, milk, Parmesan, Cheddar, garlic, and hot sauce, until well blended.

Stir in the kale and the artichoke hearts.

Spoon the mixture into a 4-cup baking dish, and bake for about 20 minutes, or until lightly golden and bubbly.

Serve warm with pita bread, tortillas, or veggies.

Tip Many artichoke products are available, from oil-packed to artichokes in a simple brine. Avoid the oil-packed artichokes for this recipe, as the extra oil will ruin the texture and add unnecessary calories.

Per Serving (½ cup) Calories: 152; Total Fat: 12g; Sodium: 207mg; Protein: 8g

Kale-Vegetable-Yogurt Dip

GLUTEN-FREES, LARGE GROUPS, SINGLETONS, 30-MINUTE, ONE POT, MAKE AHEAD

SERVES 4 / PREP: 25 MINUTES + 2 HOURS CHILLING / COOK: 0 / TOTAL: 2 HOURS, 25 MINUTES

Sometimes kids don't like to eat their vegetables, leaving parents scrambling to find ways to entice them. This creamy dip is so delicious, kids will dunk their vegetables gladly if you make a batch and put it next to a container of veggies in the refrigerator. You can include chopped fresh herbs as well, or a pinch of red pepper flakes for variety.

2 cups plain Greek yogurt

¼ cup mayonnaise

2 cups stemmed and finely chopped kale

1 scallion, finely chopped

½ red bell pepper, finely chopped

¼ cup finely chopped oil-packed sun-dried tomatoes

¼ cup finely chopped carrot

½ teaspoon minced garlic

Juice of ½ lemon

Sea salt

Freshly ground black pepper

In a large bowl, stir together the yogurt, mayonnaise, kale, scallion, red bell pepper, sun-dried tomatoes, carrot, garlic, and lemon juice, until very well mixed.

Season with sea salt and pepper.

Transfer the dip to a sealed container, and refrigerate for at least 2 hours before serving with breads, crackers, or tortilla chips.

Note **If you cannot find oil-packed sun-dried tomatoes at your market, you can create your own: In a heatproof bowl, cover regular sun-dried tomatoes with hot olive oil. When the tomatoes are plump (about 15 minutes), remove them from the cooled oil and chop them. Make sure to reserve the tomato-infused oil—it's a great flavor booster for many recipes and also makes a delicious salad dressing.**

Tip **If you want a vegan dip, use a soy or coconut yogurt without gelatin instead of standard Greek yogurt and swap out the mayonnaise for a vegan product. The texture will be slightly less creamy, but the taste will still be fantastic.**

Per Serving Calories: 208; Total Fat: 12g; Sodium: 263mg; Protein 12g

Roasted Eggplant–Kale Tapenade

SERVES 6 / PREP: 30 MINUTES / COOK: 60 MINUTES / TOTAL: 1 HOUR, 30 MINUTES

Eggplant is an acquired taste for some because it has a unique, porous texture and is often prepared incorrectly. Eggplant can also easily be overwhelmed by fat. If you use too much oil, it will soak it up like a sponge. This tapenade has a rich, complex taste, and is very versatile—it's fantastic as a sandwich spread or tossed with pasta.

1 eggplant, peeled and cut crosswise into
    ½-inch-thick slices
Sea salt
4 cups stemmed and roughly chopped kale
3 tablespoons extra-virgin olive oil, divided
2 garlic cloves, crushed
2 tomatoes, halved
½ red onion, chopped
Juice of ½ lemon
1 tablespoon balsamic vinegar
1 teaspoon chopped fresh oregano
1 teaspoon chopped fresh basil
1 tablespoon chopped fresh parsley

Preheat the oven to 350°F.

On a baking sheet, place the eggplant slices in a single layer and sprinkle with sea salt. Set aside for 15 minutes to allow the salt to draw out the moisture and bitterness from the eggplant.

Cover a second baking sheet with parchment paper.

In a large bowl, toss the kale with 1 tablespoon of olive oil until evenly coated.

Transfer the kale to the parchment-covered sheet, and spread it out evenly.

Roast the kale for about 10 minutes, or until crispy, and set aside.

Blot the eggplant with a paper towel, and add the garlic, tomatoes, and onion to the same tray.

Drizzle with the remaining 2 tablespoons of olive oil and the lemon juice.

Roast the eggplant mixture for about 50 minutes, or until the eggplant is very tender.

Let the eggplant cool.

Transfer the eggplant mixture and the roasted kale to a food processor. Add the vinegar, oregano, and basil, and pulse until the mixture is coarsely diced (the dip should have texture). Transfer the dip to a serving bowl, and garnish with the parsley.

Refrigerate, covered, until ready to serve. It will keep up to 2 days.

Note You can use aluminum foil in place of the parchment paper. Be aware, though, that parchment does not create the browning level that foil does, so there is a chance the food can burn or become too brown.

Tip Eggplant is a member of the nightshade family, which can cause issues for some people. If you have arthritis or are FODMAP (indigestible sugars) sensitive, you will have to limit your exposure to eggplant or avoid it altogether.

Per Serving Calories: 112; Total Fat: 7g; Sodium: 62mg; Protein: 3g

Mango-Kale Salsa

KIDS, VEGANS, PALEOS, GLUTEN-FREES, SINGLETONS, ONE POT

MAKES 3 CUPS / PREP: 20 MINUTES + 1 HOUR CHILLING / COOK: 0 / TOTAL: 1 HOUR, 20 MINUTES

"Salsa" usually means "tomato-based" to most people, but other fruits and vegetables can be used to create spectacular salsas, like this spicy version. If you want a milder salsa, substitute jalapeño pepper for the habanero. Add a little at a time until you reach the perfect balance between the cool cucumber, sweet mango, and hot pepper.

2 cups stemmed and chopped baby kale
1 mango, peeled and diced
½ red onion, finely diced
½ red bell pepper, finely diced
¼ English cucumber, finely diced
Zest of 1 lime
Juice of 1 lime
1 tablespoon chopped fresh cilantro
½ habanero pepper, seeded and minced
Sea salt

In a large bowl, mix together the kale, mango, onion, red bell pepper, cucumber, lime zest, lime juice, cilantro, and habanero pepper.

Season with sea salt, and transfer to a serving bowl.

Cover the bowl and place salsa in the refrigerator for 1 hour to let the flavors mingle.

Serve with tortilla chips or baked pita bread triangles.

The salsa can also be refrigerated for up to 3 days.

Tip The oils in hot peppers can be very irritating. Wear protective gloves when handling, and be careful not to touch your hands to your face or other sensitive skin.

Instead of using a paring knife to peel the mango, try a parallel vegetable peeler for a neat, efficient job.

Per Serving (½ cup) Calories: 43; Total Fat: 0g; Sodium: 50mg; Protein: 1g

Kale Guacamole

GLUTEN-FREES, LARGE GROUPS, SINGLETONS, 30-MINUTE, ONE POT

MAKES 3 CUPS / PREP: 10 MINUTES / COOK: 0 / TOTAL: 10 MINUTES

Blanched kale has an appealing bright green color. Mixed with the pale green of the avocado, the dark green chive, and cilantro, this glorious and verdant dip is the perfect summer snack. Add enough lemon juice so the avocado doesn't oxidize to an unattractive brown color. This dip is best eaten right away, but can be kept in the refrigerator overnight if you want to make it ahead.

2 cups Blanched Kale (page 33)
1 avocado, scooped from the skin
½ cup cottage cheese
2 garlic cloves, chopped
Zest of 1 lime
Juice of 1 lime
2 tablespoons chopped fresh chives
2 tablespoons chopped fresh cilantro
½ teaspoon red pepper flakes
¼ teaspoon ground cumin
Sea salt

In a food processor, blend the Blanched Kale, avocado, cottage cheese, garlic, lime zest, lime juice, chives, cilantro, red pepper flakes, and cumin, until the mixture is smooth, with little flecks of green.

Season with sea salt and serve.

Refrigerate any leftovers in a sealed container up to 3 days.

Per Serving (½ cup) Calories: 99; Total Fat: 7g; Sodium: 128mg; Protein: 4g

Kale Hummus

KIDS, VEGANS, GLUTEN-FREES, LARGE GROUPS, SINGLETONS, 30-MINUTE, ONE POT, MAKE AHEAD

MAKES 3 CUPS / PREP: 10 MINUTES / COOK: 0 / TOTAL: 10 MINUTES

Hummus is the Arabic word for *chickpea*, but this popular dip can be made with other types of beans as well as vegetables, such as cauliflower, for interesting variations. This chickpea, tahini, olive oil, and garlic-laced dip is perfect for any event and as a tasty spread for wraps and sandwiches. The kale adds a complexity and pretty green color to the dish. You can brighten this glorious green color by blanching the kale first, as long as you squeeze out any excess water to avoid a runny dip.

4 cups stemmed and coarsely chopped kale
2 cups canned chickpeas, drained and rinsed
3 garlic cloves
¼ cup tahini (sesame paste)
4 tablespoons extra-virgin olive oil
Juice of 1 lemon
¼ teaspoon sea salt

In a food processor, pulse the kale, chickpeas, garlic, tahini, olive oil, lemon juice, and sea salt until chopped.

Scrape down the sides, and purée until the mixture is smooth.

Serve with pita bread or veggies.

Store in a sealed container in the refrigerator for up to 1 week.

Tip **If you have leftover chickpeas, refrigerate them in a sealed container for up to 1 week. Use the chickpeas in salads or stews, or try roasting them in the oven for a crispy, nutritious snack.**

Per Serving (½ cup) Calories: 193; Total Fat: 15g; Sodium: 112mg; Protein: 5g

Kale-Lentil Bruschetta

LARGE GROUPS, SINGLETONS, 30-MINUTE

SERVES 12 / PREP: 15 MINUTES / COOK: 5 MINUTES / TOTAL: 20 MINUTES

Lentils add a gorgeous, almost nutty taste to this bruschetta, as well as abundant nutrients that provide health benefits. Lentils are very high in fiber, yet low in fat and calories. This combination helps lower cholesterol and stabilize blood sugar, and delivers heaps of energy to fuel your day's activities. Try this as a midafternoon snack to stave off low blood sugar slumps.

1 baguette, cut on the bias into 12 pieces, about ½ inch thick and 3 inches long
4 tablespoons extra-virgin olive oil
2 cups canned lentils, drained and rinsed
2 cups chopped Blanched Kale (page 33)
1 tomato, seeded and finely chopped
1 tablespoon finely chopped fresh basil
1 teaspoon minced garlic
¼ teaspoon sea salt
Pinch red pepper flakes
¾ cup grated Parmesan cheese, divided

Preheat the oven to broil.

Brush the bread slices with 2 teaspoons of olive oil and lay them in a single layer on a baking sheet.

Broil the bread for about 30 seconds, or until lightly toasted, watching carefully. Set aside.

In a medium bowl, mix together the remaining olive oil and the lentils, Blanched Kale, tomato, basil, garlic, sea salt, and red pepper flakes.

Spread an equal, generous amount of the kale mixture onto the toasted bread slices, and top each with 1 tablespoon of Parmesan.

Broil the bruschetta for about 1 minute, or until the cheese is lightly browned and melted, and serve.

Per Serving (1 bruschetta) Calories: 198; Total Fat: 6g; Sodium: 391mg; Protein: 9g

Berry-Kale Ice Pops

KIDS, VEGANS, PALEOS, GLUTEN-FREES, LARGE GROUPS, SINGLETONS, 30-MINUTE, ONE POT, MAKE AHEAD

MAKES 12 ICE POPS / PREP: 5 MINUTES + 4 HOURS TO FREEZE / COOK: 0 / TOTAL: 4 HOURS, 5 MINUTES

The kale's taste is almost completely lost in the assertive flavor of the berries and grape juice here, which means even kids who will not eat their kale will try these pops. You can use only blueberries if you want, but the raspberries add a certain delightful sweetness. For a more adult version, try adding fresh thyme or tarragon to the mixture before pouring it into the molds.

4 cups stemmed baby kale
1 cup frozen raspberries
1 cup frozen blueberries
1½ cups grape juice

In a blender or food processor, blend the kale, raspberries, blueberries, and grape juice until very smooth.

Pour the mixture evenly into 12 ice pop molds, and freeze for about 4 hours before serving.

Per Serving (1 ice pop) Calories: 43; Total Fat: 0g; Sodium: 6mg; Protein: 1g

Spiced Kale–Cranberry Muffins

KIDS, LARGE GROUPS, SINGLETONS, MAKE AHEAD

MAKES 12 MUFFINS / PREP: 15 MINUTES / COOK: 35 MINUTES / TOTAL: 50 MINUTES

Cranberries are a nice, tart change from the usual raisins found in most muffins, and they look like deep red rubies when you break open these muffins. Cranberries are probably best known for combating and helping prevent urinary tract infections, but they are also quite effective for strengthening the immune system and fighting inflammation in the body. Dried cranberries are an excellent source of fiber and an assortment of vitamins including A, B_6, B_{12}, C, E, and K. Use dried cranberries with no added sugar.

2 large eggs
1½ cups stemmed and very finely chopped kale
1 cup sugar
½ cup canola oil
1 tablespoon pure vanilla extract
1½ cups all-purpose flour
2 teaspoons ground cinnamon
½ teaspoon baking soda
½ teaspoon sea salt
¼ teaspoon baking powder
¼ teaspoon ground nutmeg
¼ teaspoon ground ginger
Pinch ground cloves
1 cup dried cranberries

Preheat the oven to 350°F.

Line a 12-muffin pan with paper liners and set aside.

In a large bowl, whisk together the eggs, kale, sugar, canola oil, and vanilla until well blended.

In another large bowl, stir together the flour, cinnamon, baking soda, sea salt, baking powder, nutmeg, ginger, and cloves until mixed.

Add the dry ingredients to the wet ingredients, and stir until just combined.

Fold in the cranberries.

Divide the batter evenly among the muffin cups, and bake for about 30 minutes, or until a toothpick inserted in the center of a muffin comes out clean.

Cool the muffins to room temperature on a wire rack before serving.

The muffins will keep in the refrigerator up to 5 days, or they can be frozen for 1 month.

Tip Almond flour works beautifully in this recipe in place of the all-purpose in equal amounts. This gluten-free version could be topped with slivered almonds to double up on the almond theme.

Per Serving (1 muffin) Calories: 224; Total Fat: 10g; Sodium: 146mg; Protein: 3g

Kale–Pineapple Ice Pops

KIDS, VEGANS, PALEOS, GLUTEN-FREES, LARGE GROUPS, SINGLETONS, 30-MINUTE, ONE POT, MAKE AHEAD

MAKES 12 ICE POPS / PREP: 5 MINUTES + 4 HOURS TO FREEZE / TOTAL: 4 HOURS, 5 MINUTES

Ice pops on a hot day, or after working out or playing sports, can be a lovely and refreshing treat. Commercially made ice pops are usually mostly sugar, so why buy them when homemade is so simple and nutritious? Invest in a few colorful ice pop molds, and fill them with as many tempting combinations of fruits and vegetables as you can create.

3 cups stemmed and chopped kale
2 cups diced pineapple
3 kiwis, peeled and cut into chunks
1 cup apple juice

In a blender or food processor, blend the kale, pineapple, kiwis, and apple juice until smooth.

Pour the mixture into the ice pop molds, and freeze for about 4 hours before serving.

Store pops in the molds in the freezer up to 1 month.

Tip Select pineapple by smell to get a sweet, ripe fruit. Pineapple does not continue to ripen after being picked, so if it doesn't give off a tempting, lush scent, it is not ripe enough to use.

Per Serving (1 ice pop) Calories: 43; Total Fat: 0g; Sodium: 9mg; Protein: 1g

Handy Kale Omelets

KIDS, GLUTEN-FREES, SINGLETONS, 30-MINUTE, MAKE AHEAD

SERVES 4 / PREP: 15 MINUTES / COOK: 15 MINUTES / TOTAL: 30 MINUTES

These tiny, flavorful packages look like muffins but are omelets that can be eaten as a snack when you need an energy boost. This version is cheesy, but you can also fill the muffin cups with vegetables, bits of ham or chicken, and lots of fresh herbs. Experiment until you find a family favorite.

Cooking spray
12 ounces stemmed kale, very finely chopped
4 large eggs
½ cup cottage cheese
½ cup grated sharp Cheddar cheese
1 teaspoon minced garlic
¼ teaspoon ground nutmeg
Pinch sea salt
Pinch freshly ground black pepper

Preheat the oven to 400°F.

Lightly coat 8 muffin cups with cooking spray and set aside.

In a large bowl, whisk together the kale, eggs, cottage cheese, Cheddar, garlic, nutmeg, sea salt, and pepper.

Divide the batter evenly among the muffin cups, and bake for about 15 minutes, or until set.

Let the omelets cool in the muffin pan for 5 minutes; then run a knife around the edge of each omelet and turn them out of the pan.

Serve 2 omelets per person.

Tip You can also make this recipe in a **9-by-13-inch baking dish rather than individual muffin cups, and cut the finished product into 12 pieces. The cooking time will be about 5 minutes more than for the muffins.**

Per Serving (2 omelets) Calories: 199; Total Fat: 10g; Sodium: 368mg; Protein: 16g

Kale Spanakopita Squares

KIDS, LARGE GROUPS, MAKE AHEAD

SERVES 16 / PREP: 30 MINUTES / COOK: 50 MINUTES + 25 MINUTES CHILLING AND STANDING / TOTAL: 1 HOUR, 45 MINUTES

You might be familiar with this buttery appetizer in its usual form of spinach-stuffed triangles. This recipe is easier to prepare, and the kale is a superb substitute for spinach. If you prefer to fold your spanakopita into triangles, best to watch a video online before your first attempt, as the process can be somewhat messy.

¾ cup (1½ sticks) unsalted butter, melted, plus additional for greasing
3 tablespoons extra-virgin olive oil, divided
7 cups stemmed kale, divided
4 scallions, white and green parts, chopped
2 tablespoons finely chopped fresh parsley
Sea salt
Freshly ground black pepper
2 eggs, lightly beaten
1½ cups crumbled feta cheese
2 tablespoons grated Parmesan cheese
1 teaspoon ground nutmeg
1 pound (about 20) phyllo pastry sheets

Preheat the oven to 350°F.

Brush a 9-by-13-inch baking dish with butter and set aside.

In a large skillet over medium-high heat, heat 1 tablespoon of olive oil.

Add 3½ cups of kale to the skillet, and sauté for about 6 minutes, or until it is wilted and tender. Transfer to a cutting board.

Add an additional 1 tablespoon of olive oil to the skillet and the remaining 3½ cups of kale, and sauté for about 6 minutes, or until it is wilted and tender. Transfer to the same cutting board.

Chop the kale, and squeeze out any liquid. Transfer the kale to a large bowl.

Add the remaining 1 tablespoon of olive oil to the skillet, and return the kale to the skillet.

Add the scallions and parsley, and sauté for 2 minutes. Remove from the heat.

Season the kale mixture with sea salt and pepper, and chill in the refrigerator for 10 minutes.

—→

Kale Spanakopita Squares, continued

Once the mixture is chilled, add the eggs, feta, Parmesan, and nutmeg to the kale mixture. Stir until well mixed.

Spread 10 sheets of phyllo over the bottom of the buttered baking dish, brushing each sheet with melted butter before placing the next one on top.

Spoon the kale mixture over the phyllo, spreading it evenly.

Top the kale with 10 more sheets of phyllo, brushing each sheet with melted butter before adding the next. Score the top four sheets into 16 squares with a sharp knife.

Bake for about 35 minutes, or until the top is golden.

Let the spanakopita stand 15 minutes; then cut into 16 squares and serve.

Tip **Phyllo dough, or filo, is a very thin, unleavened dough that is stretched paper-thin. It's popular for sweet pastries and appetizers like this one. The sheets you find in packages today are made using huge rollers rather than being stretched by hand.**

Per Serving (1 square) Calories: 247; Total Fat: 17g; Sodium: 400mg; Protein: 6g

Kale Potato Skins

KIDS, MEAT LOVERS, GLUTEN-FREES, LARGE GROUPS, 30-MINUTE, MAKE AHEAD

SERVES 4 / PREP: 10 MINUTES / COOK: 15 MINUTES / TOTAL: 25 MINUTES

If you want a decadent treat for Sunday football games, family get-togethers, or a backyard barbecue, try these crispy, cheesy skins. Even die-hard kale haters will love this combination of ingredients and become fans of these greens. You can also use sweet potato skins or both sweet and russet potato skins to create an interesting snack platter for a large group.

2 baked russet potatoes
1 tablespoon butter, melted
2 cups stemmed and chopped kale
¼ cup fresh basil leaves
1 teaspoon minced garlic
1 teaspoon extra-virgin olive oil
¼ cup grated Parmesan cheese
4 cooked bacon slices, chopped
1 scallion, chopped
½ cup shredded Cheddar cheese, divided

Preheat the oven to 400°F.

Cut the potatoes in half and scoop out most of the insides, leaving the skin with about ¼ inch of potato on it. Brush the skins, inside and out, with the melted butter and place on a baking sheet skin-side up.

Bake for about 7 minutes, or until crispy.

Remove from the oven and flip the skins over so the hollow part is up and set aside.

In a food processor, pulse the kale, basil, garlic, olive oil, and Parmesan until well combined and finely chopped, but still with texture.

Spoon the kale mixture evenly into the potato skins. Top each with equal amounts of bacon, scallion, and Cheddar.

Return the skins to the oven and bake for about 7 minutes, or until the cheese is bubbly and melted.

Serve warm.

Per Serving (1 potato skin) Calories: 218; Total Fat: 13g; Sodium: 332mg; Protein: 11g

Roasted Sweet Potato–Kale Couscous

VEGANS, LARGE GROUPS, SINGLETONS, MAKE AHEAD

SERVES 4 / PREP: 20 MINUTES / COOK: 20 MINUTES + 2 HOURS CHILLING / TOTAL: 2 HOURS, 40 MINUTES

When you need the perfect energy-packed snack for a busy afternoon, reach for a bowl of this lemony couscous. Sweet potato is a wonderful source of beta carotene, which has been linked to reducing the risk of certain cancers as well as promoting a healthy cardiovascular system and strong bones. You can also make this dish with butternut squash or pumpkin.

For the lemon parsley dressing
¼ cup extra-virgin olive oil
2 tablespoons freshly squeezed lemon juice
2 tablespoons chopped fresh parsley
1 teaspoon lemon zest
½ teaspoon minced garlic
Sea salt
Freshly ground black pepper

For the couscous
2 cups sweet potato, peeled and diced
1 tablespoon extra-virgin olive oil
¼ teaspoon salt
¼ teaspoon freshly ground black pepper
1 cup dried Israeli pearl couscous
4 cups stemmed and finely chopped kale
1 red pepper, finely chopped
½ red onion, peeled and finely diced
1 cup peas, fresh or frozen and thawed

To make the lemon parsley dressing:
In a medium bowl, whisk together the olive oil, lemon juice, parsley, lemon zest, and garlic until blended.

Season with sea salt and pepper and set aside.

To make the couscous:
Preheat the oven to 400°F.

Line a baking sheet with parchment paper and set aside.

In a medium bowl, toss the sweet potato with the olive oil, salt, and pepper, and transfer the vegetables to the baking sheet.

Roast the sweet potato until tender, about 20 minutes.

While the potatoes are roasting, prepare the couscous according to package directions.

Transfer the sweet potato from the baking sheet to a large bowl; add the cooked couscous, kale, red pepper, onion, and peas; and toss to combine.

Add the dressing, stir until well mixed, and season with sea salt and pepper.

Place the couscous in the fridge to chill, about 2 hours.

Serve cold or at room temperature.

Per Serving Calories: 380; Total Fat: 17g; Sodium: 261mg; Protein: 10g

6

Soups and Stews

Miso Soup with Kale

VEGANS, GLUTEN-FREES, SINGLETONS, 30-MINUTE, ONE POT

SERVES 4 / PREP: 10 MINUTES / COOK: 20 MINUTES / TOTAL: 30 MINUTES

Miso is a fermented soybean paste that can be used to create a salty, tangy soup with an Asian flair. If you want a stronger-tasting soup, use a darker miso paste. Look for this at your local Asian market or in the specialty food section of your grocery store. Miso is a complete protein, containing all the essential amino acids as well as being high in antioxidants.

6 cups vegetable broth
1 tablespoon grated peeled fresh ginger
3 tablespoons miso paste
1 teaspoon soy sauce
2 carrots, shredded
2 scallions, thinly sliced
2 cups stemmed and chopped kale

In a large stockpot over medium-high heat, bring the vegetable broth to a boil.

Add the ginger, and simmer for 4 minutes.

Add the miso paste and soy sauce, stirring to dissolve the paste. Simmer for 1 minute more.

Stir in the carrots and half of the scallions, and simmer for 2 minutes.

Add the kale. Stir the greens in the soup until they wilt and become tender, about 5 minutes.

Serve the soup topped with the remaining scallions.

Per Serving Calories: 80; Total Fat: 1g; Sodium: 743mg; Protein: 4g

Roasted Pepper–Kale Soup

VEGANS, PALEOS, GLUTEN-FREES

SERVES 4 / PREP: 15 MINUTES / COOK: 50 MINUTES / TOTAL: 1 HOUR, 5 MINUTES

This combination of smoky roasted bell peppers, sweet tomatoes, and earthy kale is sublime. The flavor of the red bell peppers and tomatoes is deepened with a splash of balsamic vinegar. Red bell peppers have been linked to treating circulation issues and reducing the risk of lung cancer. You can also use bright yellow bell peppers or orange bell peppers in this recipe, depending on what you have in your refrigerator.

10 plum tomatoes, cored, halved, and seeded
5 red bell peppers, halved and seeded
1 sweet onion, quartered
3 garlic cloves, crushed
2 celery stalks, coarsely chopped
2 tablespoons extra-virgin olive oil
2 tablespoons balsamic vinegar
6 cups vegetable broth
6 cups tightly packed stemmed and chopped kale
Sea salt
Freshly ground black pepper

Preheat the oven to 375°F.

In a large roasting pan, put the tomatoes cut-side down. Scatter the red bell peppers, onion, garlic, and celery over the tomatoes.

Drizzle the vegetables with the olive oil and balsamic vinegar.

Roast for 35 to 40 minutes, or until the vegetables are soft and slightly charred. Cool the vegetables slightly, and remove the skins from the bell peppers.

In a food processor, purée the roasted vegetables in batches with the vegetable broth and any juices from the pan.

Transfer the soup to a medium pot, and heat to a simmer.

Add the kale and simmer for about 7 minutes, or until wilted and tender.

Season with sea salt and pepper and serve.

Tip If you have a large enough roasting pan, double this recipe and freeze the extra to use as a delicious pasta sauce for another meal. If you like a chunkier sauce, pulse the roasted ingredients instead of puréeing them for a thicker texture.

Per Serving Calories: 265; Total Fat: 8g; Sodium: 329mg; Protein: 10g

Kale–Split Pea Soup

PALEOS, GLUTEN-FREES, LARGE GROUPS, SINGLETONS, ONE POT

SERVES 6 / PREP: 15 MINUTES / COOK: 1 HOUR / TOTAL: 1 HOUR, 15 MINUTES

Imagine spending a cold winter day, with the sun shimmering like jewels off the snow, making snowmen or snowshoeing on a frozen lake. Coming home to a hearty pot of split pea soup can be the perfect end to an exceptional day. You can add chunks of ham, spicy sausage slices, or chopped turkey meat to this soup to create an even more filling meal, or substitute vegetable broth and make a vegan soup instead.

1 tablespoon extra-virgin olive oil
3 celery stalks, chopped
1 sweet onion, chopped
2 teaspoons minced garlic
8 cups chicken broth
1 pound split peas, rinsed and drained
3 carrots, diced
1 tablespoon chopped fresh thyme
4 cups stemmed and chopped kale
Sea salt
Freshly ground black pepper

In a large stockpot over medium-high heat, heat the olive oil.

Add the celery, onion, and garlic, and sauté for about 4 minutes, or until softened.

Add the chicken broth and split peas to the pot, and bring the soup to a boil.

Reduce the heat to low and simmer for about 30 minutes, or until the peas are almost tender.

Add the carrots and thyme to the pot.

Simmer the soup for about 20 minutes, or until thick and the peas and vegetables are tender.

Stir in the kale and simmer for about 6 minutes, or until tender.

Season with sea salt and pepper and serve.

Per Serving Calories: 331; Total Fat: 3g; Sodium: 858mg; Protein: 22g

Broccoli—Kale Soup

GLUTEN-FREES, LARGE GROUPS, MAKE AHEAD

SERVES 6 / PREP: 15 MINUTES / COOK: 30 MINUTES / TOTAL: 45 MINUTES

Broccoli has a strong taste that is quite similar to kale, so this soup is the best of both ingredients. The finishing touch of heavy cream elevates this humble dish to a more elegant level and tones down the color to a subtle pale green. Add a sprinkle of cheese or bacon as a garnish to enhance the taste—if you don't mind a few extra calories.

1 tablespoon extra-virgin olive oil
1 sweet onion, chopped
1 teaspoon minced garlic
2 broccoli heads, chopped into florets
6 cups stemmed and chopped kale
6 cups vegetable broth
½ cup heavy cream
Juice of ½ lemon
1 teaspoon ground nutmeg
Sea salt
Freshly ground black pepper

In a large stockpot over medium-high heat, heat the olive oil.

Add the onions and garlic, and sauté for about 3 minutes, or until tender.

Add the broccoli, kale, and vegetable broth to the pot, and bring to a boil.

Reduce the heat to low, and simmer for about 20 minutes, or until the vegetables are tender.

In a food processor or blender, purée the hot soup in batches until smooth. Return the soup to the pot.

Stir in the heavy cream, lemon juice, and nutmeg, and simmer for 5 minutes.

Season with sea salt and pepper and serve.

Tip **Broccoli can keep for as long as 10 days refrigerated in a sealed bag with all the air squeezed out. When choosing broccoli, the stalks should be dry with no cracks, and the florets should be tight with no yellowing or flowering.**

Per Serving Calories: 154; Total Fat: 6g; Sodium: 242mg; Protein: 6g

Simple Turkey Meatball Soup

MEAT LOVERS, SINGLETONS, ONE POT

SERVES 4 / PREP: 20 MINUTES / COOK: 30 MINUTES / TOTAL: 50 MINUTES

Simple meatball soup accompanied by some freshly baked bread makes a welcoming family dinner or a wholesome lunch. You can add more vegetables to this soup if you want a chunkier version. The more colors in your soup, the more nutrients you're eating.

½ pound lean ground turkey
1 egg, lightly beaten
½ cup dry bread crumbs
3 tablespoons chopped fresh parsley
Pinch red pepper flakes
¼ teaspoon sea salt
1 tablespoon extra-virgin olive oil
1 sweet onion, diced
2 celery stalks, finely chopped
1 teaspoon minced garlic
1 teaspoon ground cumin
1 teaspoon ground coriander
8 cups chicken broth
8 cups stemmed and chopped kale
Sea salt
Freshly ground black pepper

In a medium bowl mix together the turkey, egg, bread crumbs, parsley, red pepper flakes, and salt. Shape into 1-inch balls and set aside.

In a large stockpot over medium-high heat, heat the olive oil.

Add the onion, celery, and garlic, and sauté for about 4 minutes, or until the vegetables are softened.

Stir in the cumin and coriander, and cook, stirring, for 1 minute.

Add the chicken broth, and bring the soup to a boil.

Add the meatballs to the simmering broth, and bring to a boil. Reduce heat, cover, and simmer for 15 minutes, or until the meat is no longer pink.

Stir in the kale and continue to simmer, stirring occasionally, for about 6 more minutes, or until the kale wilts and is tender.

Serve, seasoned with salt and pepper.

Per Serving Calories: 339; Total Fat: 12g; Sodium: 1,928mg; Protein: 27g

Leek-Potato-Kale Soup

MEAT LOVERS, GLUTEN-FREES, LARGE GROUPS

SERVES 6 / PREP: 15 MINUTES / COOK: 45 MINUTES / TOTAL: 1 HOUR

Enjoy this soup piping hot or chilled, depending on your preference and the occasion. If making a chilled soup, it is best to purée the soup until smooth and creamy rather than leaving the kale in shreds. The soup will be a fabulous green color instead of creamy white if you purée it. Add a drizzle of plain yogurt to accent the presentation.

4 bacon slices, chopped
3 leeks, trimmed, washed, and chopped
5 potatoes, peeled and diced
6 cups chicken broth
½ cup heavy cream
6 cups stemmed and shredded kale
Sea salt
Freshly ground black pepper

In a large stockpot over medium-high heat, cook the bacon for about 4 minutes, or until crispy.

Add the leeks, and sauté for about 8 minutes, or until soft and translucent.

Add the potatoes and chicken broth to the pot, and bring to a boil.

Reduce the heat to low, cover, and simmer gently for about 20 minutes, or until the potatoes are tender. Remove the soup from the heat.

In a food processor, purée the soup in batches until smooth. You can also use a handheld immersion blender to purée the entire batch in the pot.

Return the soup to the pot, and whisk in the heavy cream. Bring to a simmer, and stir in the kale. Simmer for about 5 minutes, or until tender but still brightly colored.

Season with sea salt and pepper, and serve.

Per Serving Calories: 329; Total Fat: 5g; Sodium: 764mg; Protein: 11g

Pumpkin-Kale Soup

KIDS, GLUTEN-FREES, SINGLETONS, MAKE AHEAD

SERVES 4 / PREP: 15 MINUTES / COOK: 45 MINUTES / TOTAL: 1 HOUR

Pumpkin blends well with any type of spice—from sweet to savory—so your choices are broad. This recipe uses cumin and coriander to create a warm, slightly spicy taste to accent the kale and pumpkin. You could purée the kale with the pumpkin, but you would lose the interesting appearance of green shreds in this bright soup base.

1 tablespoon butter

1 sweet onion, chopped

1 teaspoon minced garlic

6 cups chicken broth

6 cups diced pumpkin or 2 cups canned puréed pumpkin

1 teaspoon ground cumin

½ teaspoon ground coriander

Sea salt

Freshly ground black pepper

6 cups stemmed and chopped kale

¼ cup plain Greek yogurt, divided

In a large stockpot over medium-high heat, melt the butter.

Add the onion and garlic, and sauté for about 3 minutes, or until translucent.

Add the chicken broth, pumpkin, cumin, and coriander, and bring to a boil.

Reduce the heat to low, and simmer the soup for 30 to 35 minutes, or until the pumpkin is soft.

In a blender or food processor, purée the pumpkin mixture in batches, and return the soup to the pot.

Return the soup to a simmer, and season with sea salt and pepper.

Add the kale and simmer for about 6 minutes, or until wilted.

Top each serving with 1 tablespoon of yogurt and serve immediately.

Tip Several varieties of pumpkin are suitable for making soup. The best time to get a fresh pumpkin for soup is in the fall or early winter. Look for Blue Hubbard, Cinderella, or Red Kuri for your recipes.

Per Serving Calories: 215; Total Fat: 4g; Sodium: 806mg; Protein: 9g

Curried Bean & Kale Soup

GLUTEN-FREES, LARGE GROUPS, SINGLETONS, MAKE AHEAD

SERVES 4 / PREP: 15 MINUTES / COOK: 30 MINUTES / TOTAL: 45 MINUTES

Need a huge batch of soup for a potluck or for leftovers? This recipe doubles beautifully. It is so hearty and thick, you can even serve it over rice as a main course. The curry seasoning is not overly strong. If you enjoy a more assertive spice profile, adjust the amount until it's perfect.

1 tablespoon extra-virgin olive oil
2 carrots, finely diced
2 celery stalks, chopped
1 sweet potato, diced
1 sweet onion, diced
1 teaspoon minced garlic
1 teaspoon grated peeled fresh ginger
1 teaspoon ground cumin
1 teaspoon curry powder
¼ teaspoon ground paprika
¼ teaspoon red pepper flakes
6 cups low-sodium chicken broth or
    vegetable broth
½ cup tomato paste
1 cup cooked navy beans
8 cups stemmed and coarsely chopped kale
Sea salt
Freshly ground black pepper
4 teaspoons plain Greek yogurt, divided

In a large stockpot over medium-high heat, heat the olive oil.

Add the carrots, celery, sweet potato, and onion, and sauté for about 10 minutes, or until the vegetables are softened.

Add the garlic, ginger, cumin, curry powder, paprika, and red pepper flakes, and cook, stirring, for 1 minute.

Stir in the chicken broth and tomato paste, and bring the soup to a boil.

Reduce the heat to low, and simmer for about 10 minutes, or until the vegetables are cooked through.

Transfer the soup to a food processor and purée, in batches if needed.

Return the soup to the pot, add the navy beans and kale, and simmer for about 6 minutes, or until the kale is tender.

Season with sea salt and pepper. Top each serving with 1 teaspoon of yogurt and serve immediately.

Per Serving Calories: 294; Total Fat: 5g; Sodium: 696mg; Protein: 15g

Portuguese Green Soup

SERVES 4 / PREP: 10 MINUTES / COOK: 35 MINUTES / TOTAL: 45 MINUTES

Caldo Verde, a traditional Portuguese soup made with cabbage, is the inspiration for this flavorful, hearty creation. You can use any type of sausage, but chorizo or linguiça work particularly well. You can also omit the meat and use vegetable broth to make a vegan variation. Serve with thick slices of crusty bread and good company.

2 tablespoons extra-virgin olive oil
1 large sweet onion, chopped
4 teaspoons minced garlic
8 cups chicken broth or water
4 large potatoes, diced
8 ounces cooked sausage, cut into ¼-inch rounds
8 cups stemmed and finely chopped kale
Sea salt
Freshly ground black pepper

In a large stockpot over medium-high heat, heat the olive oil.

Add the onion and garlic, and sauté for about 4 minutes, or until the onion is translucent.

Add the chicken broth and potatoes, and bring the soup to a boil.

Reduce the heat to low, and simmer for about 20 minutes, or until the potatoes are extremely tender and falling apart.

Transfer the soup to a food processor and purée, in batches if needed.

Return the soup to the pot, and add the sausage. Bring to a simmer over medium heat, and cook for 3 minutes.

Add the kale, and simmer for an additional 5 minutes.

Season with sea salt and pepper, and serve immediately.

Per Serving Calories: 593; Total Fat: 24g; Sodium: 564mg; Protein: 22g

Spicy Shrimp & Kale Soup

SINGLETONS, ONE POT

SERVES 4 / PREP: 15 MINUTES / COOK: 20 MINUTES / TOTAL: 35 MINUTES

Soups featuring shrimp are usually quick to make, unless you're making a bisque, as it takes a long time to produce a perfect base from the shells. This soup can be made in under 30 minutes if you're quick (but careful) with a knife when prepping the ingredients. You can also substitute somen noodles instead of the udon if you'd prefer a thinner strand.

1 teaspoon sesame oil
1 teaspoon grated peeled fresh ginger
1 teaspoon minced garlic
6 cups low-sodium vegetable broth
1 tablespoon tamari sauce
Pinch red pepper flakes
3 ounces udon noodles or rice noodles
½ red bell pepper, thinly sliced
6 ounces shrimp, cleaned, deveined, and chopped
4 cups stemmed and chopped kale
2 scallions, sliced on the bias

In a large stockpot over medium-high heat, heat the sesame oil.

Add the ginger and garlic, and sauté for 2 minutes.

Add the vegetable broth, tamari sauce, and red pepper flakes, and bring the soup to a boil.

Add the noodles, and reduce the heat to low. Simmer for about 5 minutes, or until the noodles are soft. Add the red bell pepper and shrimp, and simmer for about 5 minutes, or just until the shrimp are pink and cooked through. Add the kale, and simmer for about 6 minutes more, or until wilted and tender.

Top with the scallions and serve.

Tip **Most mainstream grocery chains carry all the ingredients required for a basic Asian-themed recipe. If you want to try more authentic sauces, oils, and noodles, venture into an Asian market and browse the shelves. Ask the proprietor for any preparation tips that apply to ingredients you'd like to try.**

Per Serving Calories: 205; Total Fat: 3g; Sodium: 600mg; Protein: 17g

Turkey-Kale Chowder

KIDS, MEAT LOVERS, GLUTEN-FREES, LARGE GROUPS, ONE POT

SERVES 6 / PREP: 20 MINUTES / COOK: 50 MINUTES / TOTAL: 1 HOUR, 10 MINUTES

The word *chowder* somehow sounds heartier than simple soup—more crowded with ingredients and flavor. This is a correct assumption, because chowders often contain a variety of meats, vegetables, and herbs and feature a milk-thickened broth instead of plain broth. This substantial chowder has turkey meat as its protein, which makes this a wonderful recipe for using up those holiday leftovers.

2 bacon slices, chopped
1 sweet onion, chopped
2 celery stalks, chopped
2 teaspoons minced garlic
6 cups chicken broth
2 potatoes, diced
2 carrots, diced
4 cups chopped cooked turkey
½ cup heavy cream
4 cups stemmed and shredded kale
1 tablespoon chopped fresh basil
Sea salt
Freshly ground black pepper

In a large stockpot over medium-high heat, cook the bacon for about 5 minutes, or until crispy.

Add the onion, celery, and garlic, and sauté for about 3 minutes, or until translucent. Add the broth, potatoes, carrot, and turkey, and bring the soup to a boil.

Reduce the heat to low, and simmer for about 30 minutes, or until the vegetables are tender.

Stir in the heavy cream, and simmer for 2 minutes.

Stir in the kale and basil, and simmer for about 6 minutes more, or until the kale is wilted and tender.

Season with sea salt and pepper and serve.

Tip If the celery stalks you're using are from the inside of the bunch, include the greens in this soup. Those feathery ends are extremely flavorful and packed with calcium, fiber, and vitamin E.

Per Serving Calories: 294; Total Fat: 9g; Sodium: 768mg; Protein: 32g

Mediterranean Fish–Kale Chowder

PALEOS, GLUTEN-FREES, LARGE GROUPS, ONE POT

SERVES 6 / PREP: 20 MINUTES / COOK: 40 MINUTES / TOTAL: 1 HOUR

Fish chowders are usually cream based or tomato based, like this one, and have a long, colorful history as peasant food that has evolved into haute cuisine. Fish chowders were often created in cauldrons in the village's center, where each man added part of his own catch to the pot for a group celebration of a safe return from sea.

2 tablespoons extra-virgin olive oil
1 sweet onion, chopped
1 teaspoon minced garlic
2 celery stalks, chopped
2 carrots, chopped
4 cups vegetable broth or fish broth
1 (28-ounce) can sodium-free diced tomatoes
2 tablespoons tomato paste
2 bay leaves
1 teaspoon chopped fresh thyme
2 medium potatoes, peeled and diced
2 tablespoons chopped fresh parsley
Pinch cayenne pepper
Sea salt
Freshly ground black pepper
1 ½ pounds halibut or cod, cut into
   1 ½-inch pieces
6 cups chopped Blanched Kale (page 33)

In a large stockpot over medium-high heat, heat the olive oil.

Add the onions and garlic, and sauté for about 3 minutes, or until tender.

Add the celery and carrots, and sauté for 2 minutes more.

Stir in the vegetable broth, tomatoes, tomato paste, bay leaves, and thyme, and bring to a boil.

Add the potatoes, parsley, and cayenne pepper, and stir to combine.

Reduce the heat to low, and simmer for about 20 minutes, or until the potatoes are tender.

Remove the bay leaves, and season with sea salt and pepper.

Add the halibut and Blanched Kale, and continue to simmer for about 5 minutes more, or until the fish flakes with a fork. Serve.

 Tip **Check seafoodwatch.org to find more sustainable options when buying fish.**

Per Serving Calories: 323; Total Fat: 9g; Sodium: 417mg; Protein: 32g

Kale & Chickpea Stew

GLUTEN-FREES, SINGLETONS, MAKE AHEAD

SERVES 4 / PREP: 15 MINUTES / COOK: 20 MINUTES / TOTAL: 35 MINUTES

Stew usually implies a long cooking time, but you can serve this meal in just over 30 minutes. Chickpeas, also called garbanzo beans, are commonly found in Middle Eastern and Mediterranean cuisines, but they've found their way into many other types of cooking. They are extremely high in protein, fiber, and potassium while containing no cholesterol, and can be a big part of heart-friendly and diabetes-friendly diets.

1 tablespoon extra-virgin olive oil
1 sweet onion, chopped
1 tablespoon minced garlic
2 large tomatoes, chopped
1 tablespoon sweet paprika
½ teaspoon ground cumin
½ teaspoon ground coriander
Pinch cayenne pepper
4 cups chicken broth
2 (15-ounce) cans sodium-free chickpeas, drained and rinsed
Juice of 1 lemon
2 tablespoons chopped fresh cilantro
Sea salt
10 cups chopped Blanched Kale (page 33)

In a medium stockpot over medium-high heat, heat the olive oil.

Add the onion and garlic, and sauté for about 3 minutes, or until softened.

Add the tomato, paprika, cumin, coriander, and cayenne pepper, and stir together.

Stir in the chicken broth and chickpeas, and bring the soup to a boil.

Reduce the heat to low, and simmer for 10 minutes to mellow the flavors.

Transfer the soup to a food processor. Pulse, in batches if needed, until puréed but still slightly chunky. Add more broth if needed to reach desired consistency.

Return the soup to the pot, and bring back to a simmer.

Add the lemon juice and cilantro, and season with sea salt. Stir in the Blanched Kale, and simmer the soup for about 3 minutes, or until heated through but still brightly colored.

Serve immediately.

Per Serving Calories: 393; Total Fat: 7g; Sodium: 730mg; Protein: 24g

Kale–Garlic Soup
with Egg & Croutons

KIDS, SINGLETONS, 30-MINUTE

SERVES 4 / PREP: 20 MINUTES / COOK: 35 MINUTES / TOTAL: 55 MINUTES

You can make this soup appropriate for gluten-free diets by using gluten-free bread for the croutons. Take care tossing them into the oil, though, because gluten-free bread can break apart easier than regular bread. For a different presentation, you can place the poached eggs in the bottom of your soup bowls and ladle hot soup over them. This technique creates a lovely surprise for your diners when the yolk swirls to the surface of the soup.

2 cups crustless bread, cut into ½-inch cubes
6 tablespoons extra-virgin olive oil, divided
Sea salt
Freshly ground black pepper
1 teaspoon white wine vinegar
4 large eggs
1 sweet onion, peeled and chopped
2 teaspoons minced garlic
6 cups chicken stock
½ cup heavy (whipping) cream
5 cups tightly packed stemmed and chopped kale

Preheat the oven to 350°F.

Line a baking sheet with parchment paper.

In a medium bowl, toss the bread cubes with 2 tablespoons of the olive oil, and season with sea salt and pepper.

Transfer the croutons to the baking sheet, and toast in the oven, stirring once, until the croutons are golden and crisp, about 15 minutes, and set aside.

Fill a medium bowl with ice and water.

Place a 12-inch saucepan, filled with about 3 inches of water and the vinegar, over high heat. Bring to a boil, then reduce the heat to a simmer.

Reduce the heat to medium-low so the water simmers.

Break an egg into a cup, and gently tip the egg into the simmering water. Repeat with the other 3 eggs.

Turn the heat off, and cover the saucepan for 5 minutes. Using a slotted spoon, remove the eggs from the poaching water and transfer them to the ice water for 3 minutes.

➡—→

Kale-Garlic Soup with Egg & Croutons , continued

Transfer the poached eggs to a plate lined with paper towels and set aside.

In a large saucepan over medium heat, heat the remaining 4 tablespoons of olive oil.

Add the onion and garlic, and sauté until the vegetables are softened, about 3 minutes.

Add the chicken broth, and bring to a boil. Reduce the heat to low so the soup simmers.

Stir in the heavy cream and kale, and simmer for 5 minutes, until the kale is tender and wilted.

Divide the soup among four soup bowls, and top each bowl with 1 poached egg and the croutons.

Serve immediately.

Per Serving Calories: 377; Total Fat: 32g; Sodium: 1,347mg; Protein: 11g

Hearty Rice–Kale Stew

KIDS, VEGANS, GLUTEN-FREES, LARGE GROUPS, ONE POT

SERVES 6 / PREP: 15 MINUTES / COOK: 50 MINUTES / TOTAL: 1 HOUR, 5 MINUTES

Rice can add bulk and flavor to soups and stews along with an assortment of important nutrients. You can substitute white rice for the brown in this stew, but brown rice adds a distinct nutty taste. One cup of brown rice can provide the recommended daily amount of manganese, as well as good quantities of protein, selenium, and magnesium.

1 teaspoon extra-virgin olive oil
½ sweet onion, chopped
1 teaspoon minced garlic
1 (28-ounce) can crushed tomatoes
6 cups vegetable broth
1 cup brown basmati rice
2 bay leaves
2 celery stalks, diced
1 carrot, diced
1 tablespoon chopped fresh oregano
Pinch cayenne pepper
8 cups stemmed and chopped kale
Sea salt
Freshly ground black pepper
¼ cup chopped fresh parsley

In a large stockpot over medium-high heat, heat the olive oil.

Add the onion and garlic, and sauté for about 3 minutes, or until softened.

Add the crushed tomatoes, vegetable broth, rice, bay leaves, celery, and carrot, and bring to a boil.

Reduce the heat and simmer for about 35 minutes, or until the rice and vegetables are soft.

Remove the bay leaves. Stir in the oregano, cayenne pepper, and kale, and simmer for about 6 minutes, or until the kale is tender.

Season with sea salt and pepper, top with the parsley, and serve.

> **Tip** If you don't use a lot of fresh herbs in your cooking, big bunches might go to waste in your refrigerator. Try tubes of puréed fresh herbs instead. You can simply squeeze out the appropriate amount when you need it.

Per Serving Calories: 191; Total Fat: 1g; Sodium: 237mg; Protein: 6g

Tomato–Chicken–Kale Stew

MEAT LOVERS, PALEOS, GLUTEN-FREES, LARGE GROUPS, SINGLETONS, ONE POT, MAKE AHEAD

SERVES 4 / PREP: 15 MINUTES / COOK: 1 HOUR, 5 MINUTES / TOTAL: 1 HOUR, 20 MINUTES

A traditional comfort food, chicken stew sticks to the ribs and welcomes you with its lovely aroma at the end of a long day. You can make this recipe in a slow cooker as long as you add the kale at the end of the cook time, just before serving. Otherwise these greens will break down, and you will lose the texture and much of the taste.

2 teaspoons extra-virgin olive oil

3 skinless chicken breasts, cut into 1-inch chunks

1 sweet onion, chopped

3 celery stalks, chopped

2 teaspoons minced garlic

2 carrots, cut crosswise into ⅛-inch-thick slices

1 cup low-sodium chicken broth

4 tomatoes, coarsely chopped

½ cup oil-packed sun-dried tomatoes, chopped

4 cups stemmed and chopped kale

2 teaspoons chopped fresh thyme

Pinch red pepper flakes

Sea salt

Freshly ground black pepper

In a large stockpot over medium-high heat, heat the olive oil.

Add the chicken and sauté for about 5 minutes, or until lightly browned and partially cooked through. Using a slotted spoon, transfer the chicken to a plate. Set aside.

Place the pot back over the heat. Add the onion, celery, garlic, and carrots, and sauté for about 5 minutes, or until the vegetables are crisp-tender.

Add the chicken back to the pot, along with any accumulated juices on the plate.

Add the chicken broth, tomatoes, and sun-dried tomatoes, and bring to a boil.

Reduce the heat to low, cover the pot, and simmer for about 45 minutes, or until the chicken and vegetables are tender.

Stir in the kale, thyme, and red pepper flakes, and simmer for about 6 minutes, or until the kale is wilted and tender.

Season with sea salt and pepper, and serve.

Per Serving Calories: 364; Total Fat: 12g; Sodium: 523mg; Protein: 42g

Beef, Bacon & Kale Stew

KIDS, MEAT LOVERS, PALEOS, GLUTEN-FREES, LARGE GROUPS, ONE POT, MAKE AHEAD

SERVES 8 / PREP: 15 MINUTES / COOK: 4 HOURS / TOTAL: 4 HOURS, 15 MINUTES

Simple and satisfying, flavorful beef, salty bacon, and tender shredded kale produce an exceptional dish that can be doubled and frozen for future meals. If you want to freeze this stew, omit the kale, adding it when you reheat the stew to serve. You can also spoon the stew into a pie shell to create a tasty pot pie.

4 ounces bacon, chopped
1 (1-pound) beef chuck roast, trimmed of excess fat and cut into ½-inch chunks
1 sweet onion, chopped
2 teaspoons minced garlic
1 cup red wine
4 cups beef broth
3 carrots, finely diced
2 potatoes, cut into ½-inch dice
2 teaspoons chopped fresh thyme
5 cups stemmed and chopped kale
Sea salt
Freshly ground black pepper

In a large stockpot over medium-high heat, cook the bacon for about 5 minutes, or until crispy. Using a slotted spoon, transfer the bacon to a plate and set aside.

Add the beef chunks to the pot, and brown the beef in the bacon fat for 5 minutes. Using a slotted spoon, transfer the beef to the same plate with the bacon and set aside. Add the onion and garlic to the pot, and sauté for about 3 minutes, or until softened.

Add the red wine and deglaze the pot, scraping up any browned bits on the bottom.

Add the beef broth, bacon, browned beef and any accumulated juices on the plate, carrots, potatoes, and thyme to the pot. Bring the stew to a boil.

Reduce the heat to low and simmer for about 3½ hours, or until the beef is very tender. Stir in the kale and simmer for another 6 minutes. Season with sea salt and pepper and serve.

 Tip Thyme is high in vitamin K, iron, healthy volatile oils, and potassium.

Per Serving Calories: 389; Total Fat: 22g; Sodium: 654mg; Protein: 25g

Chorizo & Kale Stew

MEAT LOVERS, GLUTEN-FREES, LARGE GROUPS, ONE POT

SERVES 6 / PREP: 20 MINUTES / COOK: 30 MINUTES / TOTAL: 50 MINUTES

Chorizo is a sausage found in Latin America and Spain. It gets its signature red color from the large amounts of paprika used in its preparation. You can use spicy or sweet chorizo in this recipe, although the hotter version plays up the flavor of the other ingredients nicely. Chorizo is a cured meat, fully cooked, so you only need brown it lightly and remove it from the pan rather than cook the meat completely from a raw stage. If you cannot find chorizo, you can substitute hot Italian sausage; however, you must cook it completely as it is a raw product.

1 tablespoon extra-virgin olive oil

1¼ pounds chorizo, halved and cut into ½-inch chunks

3 large sweet potatoes, diced

1 sweet onion, chopped

2 teaspoons minced garlic

1½ teaspoons smoked paprika

10 cups stemmed and chopped kale

6 cups chicken broth

2 cups cooked white beans

Sea salt

Freshly ground black pepper

¼ cup grated Parmesan cheese

In a large stockpot over medium-high heat, heat the olive oil.

Add the chorizo and cook for about 4 minutes, or until lightly browned and the fat renders. Using a slotted spoon, transfer the sausage to a plate and set aside. Add the sweet potatoes, onion, and garlic to the pot, and sauté for about 6 minutes, or until lightly browned.

Add the paprika, and sauté 1 minute more.

Stir in the kale, tossing with tongs until wilted, about 5 minutes.

Stir in the reserved chorizo, chicken broth, and beans, and bring the soup to a boil.

Reduce the heat to low and simmer for about 10 minutes, or until the vegetables are tender.

Season with sea salt and pepper.

Top with the Parmesan and serve.

Per Serving Calories: 806; Total Fat: 42g; Sodium: 2,091mg; Protein: 40g

Venison-Kale Stew

MEAT LOVERS, PALEOS, GLUTEN-FREES, LARGE GROUPS, ONE POT, MAKE AHEAD

SERVES 6 / PREP: 20 MINUTES / COOK: 2 HOURS, 15 MINUTES / TOTAL: 2 HOURS, 35 MINUTES

Venison, not often the first choice for a flavorful, hearty stew, cooks up tender and tasty, and it freezes perfectly for leftovers. While many do hunt their own deer, there are also many commercial farms today that raise these animals. The deer spend most of their time grazing in pastures, so many animal welfare consumers prefer this meat to beef.

1 tablespoon extra-virgin olive oil
1 pound venison, cut into ½-inch chunks
5 celery stalks, chopped
1 sweet onion, chopped
2 teaspoons minced garlic
3 sweet potatoes, cut into ½-inch chunks
3 carrots, cut crosswise into ¼-inch-thick slices
4 cups beef broth
1 cup dry red wine
1 (5-ounce) can tomato paste
2 bay leaves
2 teaspoons chopped fresh rosemary
6 cups stemmed and chopped kale
Sea salt
Freshly ground black pepper

In a large stockpot over medium-high heat, heat the olive oil.

Add the venison and brown for 5 minutes. Using a slotted spoon, transfer the meat to a plate and set aside.

Add the celery, onion, and garlic to the pot, and sauté for about 4 minutes, or until softened.

Add the sweet potatoes, carrots, reserved meat with any accumulated juices on the plate, beef broth, red wine, tomato paste, bay leaves, and rosemary to the pot. Bring the stew to a boil.

Reduce the heat to low, and simmer for about 2 hours, or until the stew has thickened.

Remove the bay leaves, and stir in the kale. Simmer for about 6 minutes, or until the kale is tender.

Season with sea salt and pepper and serve.

Tip Venison is a very lean meat that doesn't have to be trimmed of fat like beef or lamb. You might have to add fat to the dish, such as bacon grease or lard, to get the right texture.

Per Serving Calories: 342; Total Fat: 4g; Sodium: 469mg; Protein: 30g

Lamb Stew with Kale

MEAT LOVERS, PALEOS, GLUTEN-FREES, LARGE GROUPS, ONE POT, MAKE AHEAD

SERVES 4 / PREP: 15 MINUTES / COOK: 55 MINUTES / TOTAL: 1 HOUR, 10 MINUTES

Lamb is a staple meat in Northern Africa, Australia, and New Zealand because these regions cannot always support the demands of cattle. Since it is not a commonly used ingredient in most North American home kitchens, this stew is an easy way to start incorporating healthy lamb into your diet. Ground lamb is less intimidating than whole cuts of meat. You can use chunks of lamb instead, but increase the cooking time by at least 45 minutes.

2 teaspoons extra-virgin olive oil

12 ounces ground lamb

1 sweet onion, chopped

2 teaspoons minced garlic

1 teaspoon grated peeled fresh ginger

2 cups diced butternut squash

2 carrots, finely diced

1 (28-ounce) can sodium-free crushed tomatoes

4 cups chicken broth

2 teaspoons smoked paprika

1 teaspoon ground cumin

½ teaspoon ground coriander

Sea salt

5 cups stemmed and chopped kale

In a large stockpot over medium-high heat, heat the olive oil.

Add the lamb and sauté for about 6 minutes, or until cooked through.

Add the onion, garlic, and ginger, and sauté for about 3 minutes, or until the vegetables are softened.

Add the butternut squash, carrots, tomatoes, chicken broth, paprika, cumin, and coriander, and bring the stew to a boil.

Reduce the heat to low and simmer for about 35 minutes, or until the vegetables are tender.

Season with sea salt.

Stir in the kale and simmer for 6 minutes more, or until the kale is wilted and tender.

Serve hot.

Tip If you look at old recipes for lamb stew, you might be surprised at the very long cooking times. These stews, often made with the tougher meat from older animals, needed hours of braising to become palatable and tender. Lamb today is butchered younger and so requires less time in the oven or on the stove.

Per Serving Calories: 460; Total Fat: 9g; Sodium: 895mg; Protein: 36g

7

Salads Galore

Kale Salad
with Smoked Salmon & Avocado

GLUTEN-FREES, 30-MINUTE

SERVES 4 / PREP: 15 MINUTES / COOK: 0 / TOTAL: 15 MINUTES

Smoked salmon, which used to be a luxury item purchased only from gourmet food stores, can now be found in supermarket seafood sections. It is an incredible ingredient in scrambled eggs, dips, pastas, and as an accent on salads like this one. Smoked salmon has all the nutritional benefits of fresh fish but can deliver a high dose of sodium—so go light on the amount if your diet is sodium-restricted.

For the dressing
½ cup extra-virgin olive oil
¼ cup freshly squeezed lemon juice
¼ cup chopped fresh dill
1 teaspoon lemon zest
Sea salt
Freshly ground black pepper

For the salad
6 cups stemmed and chopped kale
1 pound smoked salmon, chopped
1 avocado, cut into ¼-inch dice
1 mango, cut into ¼-inch dice
½ cup chopped red onion
¼ cup crumbled feta cheese, divided
¼ cup chopped pecans, divided

To make the dressing:
In a small bowl, whisk together the olive oil, lemon juice, dill, and lemon zest.

Season with sea salt and pepper and set aside.

To make the salad:
In a large bowl, toss together the kale, salmon, avocado, mango, and red onion until mixed well.

Arrange the salad, evenly divided, on 4 plates. Drizzle each salad with an equal amount of dressing.

Top each salad with 1 tablespoon of feta and 1 tablespoon of pecans, and serve.

Per Serving Calories: 571; Total Fat: 45g; Sodium: 2,487mg; Protein: 27g

Kale-Chicken-Lentil Salad
with Tomato Vinaigrette

MEAT LOVERS, GLUTEN-FREES, LARGE GROUPS, SINGLETONS, 30-MINUTE, MAKE AHEAD

SERVES 4 / PREP: 20 MINUTES / COOK: 0 / TOTAL: 20 MINUTES

Use up leftover roasted chicken in this filling salad—either breast meat or dark meat, depending on what's in your refrigerator. When you make roasted chicken, make a large one, or more than one, so you'll have cooked chicken available for other recipes. Strip the meat from the bones and either refrigerate it or freeze it in portioned bags.

For the vinaigrette
½ tomato, seeded and chopped
4 oil-packed sun-dried tomatoes, chopped
2 tablespoons balsamic vinegar
½ teaspoon minced garlic
½ cup extra virgin olive oil
Sea salt
Freshly ground black pepper

For the salad
6 cups bite-size stemmed kale pieces
2 cups halved cherry tomatoes
1 cup cooked lentils
1 cup chopped cooked chicken breast
2 tablespoons chopped fresh basil, divided

To make the vinaigrette:
In a blender, pulse the tomato, sun-dried tomatoes, balsamic vinegar, and garlic for about 30 seconds, or until finely chopped.

Add the olive oil and blend until smooth.

Season with sea salt and pepper and set aside.

To make the salad:
In a large bowl, toss together the kale, cherry tomatoes, lentils, and chicken until mixed well.

Add the dressing and toss to coat.

Evenly divide the salad among 4 plates, top each with 1½ teaspoons of basil, and serve.

Tip Look for quality balsamic vinegar for your dressings. It can make a real difference in the taste of the finished recipe. Balsamic vinegar is a centuries-old industry in many countries, with casks aged over 25 years in some areas. You can even enjoy a small glass of exceptional balsamic vinegar like a fine liqueur.

Per Serving Calories: 406; Total Fat: 27g; Sodium: 309mg; Protein: 21g

Warm Kale-Potato Salad

VEGANS, PALEOS, GLUTEN-FREES, LARGE GROUPS, MAKE AHEAD

SERVES 4 / PREP: 20 MINUTES / COOK: 20 MINUTES / TOTAL: 40 MINUTES

Mayonnaise- and egg-drenched potato salads are probably what you're most familiar with, so this lightly herbed, vinaigrette-dressed salad will be a lovely variation to try. The trick to a flavorful salad is to toss the potatoes with the dressing when warm. You can also serve this salad as a side dish.

For the dressing
¼ cup extra-virgin olive oil
2 tablespoons balsamic vinegar
1 teaspoon Dijon mustard
½ teaspoon minced garlic
Sea salt
Freshly ground black pepper

For the salad
4 cups water
Pinch sea salt
7 cups stemmed and coarsely chopped kale
1 pound baby potatoes, scrubbed and cut into ½-inch chunks
2 scallions, chopped
2 tablespoons chopped fresh parsley

To make the dressing:
In a small bowl, whisk together the olive oil, balsamic vinegar, mustard, and garlic.

Season with sea salt and pepper and set aside.

To make the salad:
In a large pot over medium-high heat, bring the water and sea salt to a boil.

Add the kale and potatoes to the pot, cover, and reduce the heat to medium.

Simmer for about 15 minutes, or until the greens and potatoes are tender.

Remove from the heat, drain, and transfer the kale and potatoes to a large bowl.

Add the scallions and dressing, and toss to coat.

Top with the parsley and serve.

Tip Baby, or new, potatoes are root vegetables taken out of the soil before they are fully grown. They have thinner skin and an almost sweet, creamy interior. Examine each baby potato carefully to ensure that none has a green pigment on its skin. This pigment, called solanine, is toxic.

Per Serving Calories: 236; Total Fat: 13g; Sodium: 136mg; Protein: 7g

Lemon–Kale Salad
with Apples & Blue Cheese

GLUTEN-FREES, SINGLETONS, 30-MINUTE

SERVES 4 / PREP: 25 MINUTES / COOK: 0 / TOTAL: 25 MINUTES

An apple a day really can keep the doctor away because they contain almost all the essential vitamins and minerals, in some quantity, making them juicy, delicious multivitamins. Apples are available year-round, but when possible, find a pick-it-yourself orchard and experience an apple warmed by the autumn sun when they're in season.

For the dressing
2 tablespoons freshly squeezed lemon juice
1 tablespoon extra-virgin olive oil
1 teaspoon honey
½ teaspoon chopped fresh thyme
Pinch sea salt
Pinch freshly ground black pepper

For the salad
6 cups stemmed and torn kale
2 celery stalks, thinly sliced
1 apple, cored and diced
1 scallion, thinly sliced on the bias
2 ounces crumbled blue cheese, divided
2 tablespoons chopped pecans, divided

To make the dressing:
In a small bowl, whisk together the lemon juice, olive oil, honey, and thyme.

Season with sea salt and pepper and set aside.

To make the salad:
In a large bowl, toss together the kale and dressing. Let stand for 10 minutes.

Evenly divide the kale among 4 plates. Top each salad with equal amounts of the celery, apple, scallion, blue cheese, and pecans.

Serve immediately.

Tip For the best quality, shell your own pecans rather than buying chopped products in bulk bins or packages. Pecans turn rancid easily, so if you have to buy bulk nuts, taste one to check for its signature buttery sweet flavor rather than any bitterness. Store extra pecans in the freezer to preserve their flavor.

Per Serving Calories: 212; Total Fat: 13g; Sodium: 309mg; Protein: 7g

Kale Salad
with Warm Bacon Dressing

KIDS, MEAT LOVERS, GLUTEN-FREES, 30-MINUTE

SERVES 4 / PREP: 20 MINUTES / COOK: 5 MINUTES / TOTAL: 25 MINUTES

Warm bacon dressing is simple to make and absolutely addictive. This is not a dressing that can sit, so don't make it until you're ready to serve the salad. If the bacon doesn't render at least four tablespoons of fat, add enough olive oil to make up the difference so your dressing is balanced.

For the dressing
8 bacon slices, chopped
4 tablespoons apple cider vinegar
1 teaspoon Dijon mustard
Sea salt
Freshly ground black pepper

For the salad
1 tablespoon butter
2 cups sliced white mushrooms
6 cups stemmed and chopped kale
¼ cup crumbled blue cheese

To make the dressing:
In a small skillet over medium-high heat, cook the bacon for about 5 minutes, or until crispy.

Remove the skillet from the heat. Using a slotted spoon, transfer the bacon to a plate and set aside.

Pour the bacon fat from the skillet into a small bowl.

Whisk in the cider vinegar and mustard.

Season with sea salt and pepper.

To make the salad:
In a small skillet over medium-high heat, melt the butter.

Sauté the mushrooms in the butter until golden brown, about 5 minutes.

In a large bowl, toss the kale with the warm dressing until the greens wilt slightly.

Evenly divide the kale among 4 plates. Top each with an equal amount of mushrooms, blue cheese crumbles, and bacon and serve.

Per Serving Calories: 266; Total Fat: 9g; Sodium: 535mg; Protein: 14g

Kale Tabbouleh

VEGANS, PALEOS, GLUTEN-FREES, LARGE GROUPS, SINGLETONS, 30-MINUTE, MAKE AHEAD

SERVES 4 / PREP: 30 MINUTES / COOK: 0 / TOTAL: 30 MINUTES

Tabbouleh usually includes copious amounts of finely chopped herbs. In this dish, kale is used instead. Quinoa replaces the traditional bulgur, or couscous, here adding all nine essential amino acids, as quinoa is a complete protein. It also has a higher amount of protein than eggs and most other grains and is an excellent source of fiber, calcium, and iron.

For the dressing
Juice of 1 lemon
¼ cup extra-virgin olive oil
Sea salt
Freshly ground black pepper

For the salad
6 cups stemmed and finely chopped kale
½ cup fresh parsley, finely chopped
1 cup cooked quinoa
2 tomatoes, seeded and chopped
½ English cucumber, chopped
½ red onion, chopped

To make the dressing:
In a small bowl, whisk together the lemon juice and olive oil.

Season with sea salt and pepper and set aside.

To make the salad:
In a large bowl, toss together the kale, parsley, quinoa, tomatoes, cucumber, and red onion.

Add the dressing, toss until well mixed, and serve.

Per Serving Calories: 259; Total Fat: 14g; Sodium: 110mg; Protein: 7g

Broccoli & Kale Salad
with Hot Honey-Mustard Dressing

PALEOS, GLUTEN-FREES, SINGLETONS, 30-MINUTE

SERVES 4 / PREP: 15 MINUTES / COOK: 0 / TOTAL: 15 MINUTES

Mustard dressing is versatile and can be used for many salads besides this one. Double or triple the recipe, and refrigerate the extra in a sealed container up to one month. If you want a hotter dressing, use a spicy English mustard instead of Dijon and adjust the amount of jalapeño to your taste.

For the dressing
¼ cup extra-virgin olive oil
2 tablespoons Dijon mustard
Juice of 1 lime
2 tablespoons honey
¼ teaspoon minced garlic
½ jalapeño pepper, seeded
Sea salt
Freshly ground black pepper

For the salad
6 cups stemmed and shredded kale
2 broccoli heads, finely chopped
1 cup shredded carrot
2 cups halved red grapes
½ cup chopped almonds

To make the dressing:
In a blender, pulse the olive oil, mustard, lime juice, honey, garlic, and jalapeño until smooth.

Season with sea salt and pepper and set aside.

To make the salad:
In a large bowl, toss together the kale, broccoli, carrot, and grapes with the dressing until very well mixed.

Garnish with the almonds and serve.

> **Tip** **If you want a more fiery dressing, don't seed the jalapeño. The seeds and ribs in these pretty peppers contain most of the heat. Because the pepper's hot oil can severely irritate any mucous membrane, wear protective gloves and avoid touching your hands to your face, eyes, or other sensitive skin, and always wash your hands very well after handling any type of hot pepper.**

Per Serving Calories: 341; Total Fat: 19g; Sodium: 248mg; Protein: 10g

Kale–Grapefruit Salad
with Zesty Citrus Dressing

VEGANS, PALEOS, GLUTEN-FREES, SINGLETONS, 30-MINUTE

SERVES 4 / PREP: 20 MINUTES / COOK: 0 / TOTAL: 20 MINUTES

Ruby red grapefruit is the best choice here instead of white grapefruit. The rosy-hued fruit is sweeter and looks gorgeous on the dark green kale. Grapefruit is high in vitamins A and C, calcium, pectin, potassium, and beta-carotene. This tart fruit can reduce the risk of cancer and osteoporosis while also stimulating digestion.

For the dressing
¼ cup extra-virgin olive oil
2 tablespoons freshly squeezed orange juice
1 tablespoon apple cider vinegar
Zest of 1 lime
Juice of 1 lime
1 tablespoon chopped fresh cilantro
Pinch cayenne pepper
Sea salt
Freshly ground black pepper

For the salad
6 cups stemmed and finely chopped kale
2 ruby red grapefruits, peeled, pith removed, and segmented
1 avocado, chopped
½ red onion, thinly sliced

To make the dressing:
In a small bowl, whisk together the olive oil, orange juice, cider vinegar, lime zest, lime juice, cilantro, and cayenne pepper.

Season with sea salt and pepper and set aside.

To make the salad:
In a large bowl, toss the kale together with half of the dressing until well mixed.

Evenly divide the kale among 4 plates. Top each salad with equal amounts of grapefruit, avocado, and onion.

Evenly drizzle the remaining dressing over the salads and serve.

Tip You can section grapefruit by simply peeling them and taking apart the segments with the membranes still intact. However, you can easily create pretty segments, called suprêmes, by completely cutting off all the skin and pith before cutting out the individual sections between the membranes. Squeeze the juice out of the empty membranes into your dressing for a citrusy boost.

Per Serving Calories: 301; Total Fat: 22g; Sodium: 113mg; Protein: 4g

Summer Fresh Kale Salad
with Mint Dressing

KIDS, GLUTEN-FREES, LARGE GROUPS, SINGLETONS, 30-MINUTE

SERVES 4 / PREP: 30 MINUTES / COOK: 0 / TOTAL: 30 MINUTES

What would a summer salad be without sweet, bright corn kernels cut right from the cob? Although fresh is best, sometimes time constraints or product availability can determine what you use. Cutting kernels off the cob can take time you might not have, so in a pinch, use a high-quality flash-frozen corn product. Simply thaw the corn and add it to your salad.

For the dressing
¼ cup extra-virgin olive oil
3 tablespoons white balsamic vinegar
1 tablespoon chopped fresh mint
2 teaspoons minced scallion
1 teaspoon minced jalapeño pepper
Sea salt
Freshly ground black pepper

For the salad
6 cups stemmed and chopped kale
2 nectarines, thinly sliced
2 plums, thinly sliced
1 cup fresh corn kernels
2 ounces goat cheese, crumbled
½ cup pea shoots (optional)

To make the dressing:
In a small bowl, whisk together the olive oil, white balsamic vinegar, mint, scallion, and jalapeño. Season with sea salt and pepper and set aside.

To make the salad:
In a large bowl, toss together the kale and about two-thirds of the dressing until well mixed.

Evenly divide the kale among 4 plates. Top each salad with one-fourth of the nectarine slices and plums and ¼ cup of corn.

Drizzle with equal amounts of the remaining dressing, top each salad with equal amounts of goat cheese and the pea shoots (if using) and crumbled goat cheese, and serve.

Tip **Nectarines are often overlooked in favor of their more flamboyantly fragrant, fuzzy cousin—peaches. However, nectarines are the perfect complement to kale in this recipe because their firmer flesh will not get mushy when tossed with the other ingredients and the dressing.**

Per Serving Calories: 287; Total Fat: 18g; Sodium: 152mg; Protein: 9g

Roasted Root Vegetable & Kale Salad

VEGANS, PALEOS, GLUTEN-FREES, LARGE GROUPS, SINGLETONS

SERVES 4 / PREP: 20 MINUTES / COOK: 35 MINUTES / TOTAL: 1 HOUR, 10 MINUTES

Vegetables get lightly caramelized and sweet when roasted and lightly seasoned with just a touch of salt and pepper. Celeriac is a pale root ball that might look dirty and strange in the supermarket, but it tastes like celery and has a pleasing firm texture. Use any leftover celeriac in a stew, mashed in a side dish, or shredded in a salad.

1 sweet potato, cut into ½-inch dice
3 parsnips, cut into ½-inch pieces
½ celeriac, peeled and cut into ½-inch pieces
1 tablespoon extra-virgin olive oil, divided
Sea salt
Freshly ground black pepper
½ teaspoon minced garlic
5 cups stemmed and coarsely chopped kale
Juice of ½ lemon
½ cup almonds, roughly chopped
Parmesan cheese, to serve

Preheat the oven to 400°F.

In a large bowl, toss together the sweet potato, parsnips, carrot, and celeriac with 2 teaspoons of olive oil to coat. Season lightly with sea salt and pepper.

Transfer the vegetables to a baking dish, and roast for about 30 minutes, or until tender and lightly caramelized, turning once. Transfer the vegetables to a large bowl, and set aside to cool for 15 minutes.

In a large skillet over medium-high heat, heat the remaining 1 teaspoon of olive oil. Add the garlic and sauté until fragrant, about 1 minute. Add the kale and toss with tongs until just wilted, about 4 minutes.

Remove the skillet from the heat, and transfer the kale to the bowl with the vegetables. Sprinkle with the lemon juice, add almonds, and toss well. Serve with freshly grated Parmesan cheese.

 Tip Look for slender, smaller parsnips because the larger ones can be woody and almost bitter in taste.

Per Serving Calories: 186; Total Fat: 4g; Sodium: 200mg; Protein: 5g

Kale-Mango Salad
with Creamy Avocado Dressing

KIDS, GLUTEN-FREES, LARGE GROUPS, 30-MINUTE

SERVES 4 / PREP: 30 MINUTES / COOK: 0 / TOTAL: 30 MINUTES

Mangoes are often used in sweet dishes but are equally at home in savory recipes, especially here, paired with rich avocado and assertive greens. The vibrant color of this lush fruit indicates it is very high in antioxidants, such as beta carotene. Mango is also high in amino acids, calcium, iron, and vitamins A and C. If you want to add interesting texture to this salad, try using a shredded, slightly green mango as well as a ripe one.

For the dressing
½ cup buttermilk
½ avocado
1 garlic clove
1 tablespoon freshly squeezed lemon juice
1 teaspoon onion powder
½ teaspoon sweet paprika
2 tablespoons chopped fresh dill
Sea salt
Freshly ground black pepper

For the salad
6 cups stemmed and chopped kale
2 cups baby spinach
2 mangoes, peeled and diced
½ avocado, chopped
½ jicama, julienned
1 scallion, thinly sliced on the bias

To make the dressing:
In a blender, pulse the buttermilk, avocado, garlic, lemon juice, onion powder, sweet paprika, and dill until very smooth.

Season with sea salt and pepper and set aside.

To make the salad:

In a large bowl, toss together the kale, spinach, and half of the dressing until well coated.

Transfer the greens to a large serving dish, and top with the mango chunks, avocado, jicama, and scallions.

Drizzle the remaining dressing over the salad and serve.

Tip **The simplest method of creating julienned jicama is with a mandoline. This kitchen tool uses parallel and perpendicular blades to create batons, matchsticks and julienned and cross-hatched vegetables, which can be a huge time saver, even if you are very good with a knife.**

Per Serving Calories: 229; Total Fat: 11g; Sodium: 227mg; Protein: 9g

Hearty Kale–Barley Salad
with Fig & Balsamic Dressing

LARGE GROUPS, SINGLETONS, 30-MINUTE, MAKE AHEAD

SERVES 4 / PREP: 30 MINUTES / COOK: 0 / TOTAL: 30 MINUTES

Barley is perfect for salads, with its pleasing chewy texture and interesting nutty taste. You'll find several types of barley on your grocer's shelves, but the most nutritious choice is hulled barley, which needs a little longer to cook. If you purchase barley from bulk bins, make sure it's in covered containers and that the store has a good turnover rate.

For the dressing
4 ripe figs (do not substitute dried)
¼ cup balsamic vinegar
1 tablespoon freshly squeezed lemon juice
1 tablespoon honey
½ cup extra-virgin olive oil
Sea salt
Freshly ground black pepper

For the salad
6 cups stemmed and shredded kale
2 cups halved cherry tomatoes
1 cup cooked barley
2 scallions, chopped
¼ cup pumpkin seeds
½ cup crumbled feta cheese

To make the dressing:
In a blender, pulse the figs, balsamic vinegar, lemon juice, and honey until smooth.

With the blender on a medium setting, slowly add the olive oil in a thin stream, processing until the dressing is emulsified.

Season with sea salt and pepper, and set aside.

To make the salad:
In a large bowl, toss together the kale, cherry tomatoes, barley, and scallions until well mixed.

Add the dressing, toss to coat, and transfer the salad to a large serving dish.

Top with the pumpkin seeds and feta, and serve.

 Tip Before cooking the barley, pick through it carefully for stones and then rinse the grains thoroughly. You don't want to chip a tooth on unwelcome inedible ingredients in your salad.

Per Serving Calories: 513; Total Fat: 34g; Sodium: 320mg; Protein: 12g

Kale-Orange Salad
with Lime-Honey Dressing

KIDS, PALEOS, GLUTEN-FREES, LARGE GROUPS, 30-MINUTE

SERVES 4 / PREP: 10 MINUTES / COOK: 0 / TOTAL: 10 MINUTES

This salad looks stunning, especially with the bright red of the cabbage on the deep green of the kale. Other types of cabbage would also be effective for this salad, but try to get a contrast in colors for the appearance. Delicate shredded Napa cabbage would add pale green, and the creamy white of shredded bok choy could be a visual delight.

For the dressing
Juice of 1 lime
1 tablespoon honey
¼ cup extra-virgin olive oil
Sea salt
Freshly ground black pepper

For the salad
6 cups stemmed and chopped kale
2 oranges, peeled and segmented
1 avocado, chopped
1 cup shredded red cabbage
½ cup chopped hazelnuts

To make the dressing:
In a small bowl, whisk together the lime juice, honey, and olive oil until well blended.

Season with sea salt and pepper and set aside.

To make the salad:
In a large bowl, toss the kale with the dressing until evenly coated.

Evenly divide the kale among 4 plates. Top each with equal amounts of the oranges, avocado, red cabbage, and hazelnuts, and serve.

Tip **Lemons are considered vitamin C powerhouses, but the smaller lime has even more of this important vitamin. This is why limes were taken in bushels aboard ships on the high seas to stave off scurvy in sailors.**

Per Serving Calories: 418; Total Fat: 31g; Sodium: 154mg; Protein: 10g

Shredded Kale Greek Salad

KIDS, GLUTEN-FREES, LARGE GROUPS, SINGLETONS, 30-MINUTE

SERVES 4 / PREP: 20 MINUTES / COOK: 0 / TOTAL: 20 MINUTES

If you like traditional Greek salad with romaine lettuce, this kale variation might just become a new favorite. The kale's flavor is more assertive than romaine, and it stays crisp as the next day's leftovers. The kale gets lightly pickled in this dressing and tastes great stuffed into a pita bread with some chicken.

For the dressing
½ cup extra-virgin olive oil
4 tablespoons balsamic vinegar
2 tablespoons chopped fresh oregano
Pinch of red pepper flakes
Sea salt
Freshly ground black pepper

For the salad
6 cups stemmed and shredded kale
¼ English cucumber, julienned
1 carrot, julienned
1 cup crumbled feta cheese
¼ cup dried cranberries
¼ cup pine nuts

To make the dressing:
In a small bowl, whisk together the olive oil, balsamic vinegar, oregano, and red pepper flakes.

Season with sea salt and pepper and set aside.

To make the salad:
In a large bowl, toss together the kale and the dressing until well mixed.

Evenly divide the kale mixture among 4 plates. Top each salad with equal amounts of the julienned cucumber and carrot, ¼ cup of feta, 1 tablespoon dried cranberries, and 1 tablespoon pine nuts and serve.

Tip English cucumbers are more expensive than regular cucumbers but are worth it when you consider the taste and texture. Since the peel on English cucumbers is thin, you can leave it on, and the flesh is sweet with tiny edible seeds. Regular cucumbers often have to be peeled and seeded before you can use them.

Per Serving Calories: 419; Total Fat: 35g; Sodium: 673mg; Protein: 10g

Kale–Couscous Salad
with Ginger Vinaigrette

VEGANS, LARGE GROUPS, SINGLETONS, 30-MINUTE, MAKE AHEAD

SERVES 4 / PREP: 30 MINUTES / COOK: 0 / TOTAL: 30 MINUTES

Couscous looks like a grain, but it's pasta made from semolina. Israeli couscous is also called pearl couscous and is larger than the regular type. This means it's chewier and less fluffy, but with a delicious nutty flavor. Cook this product in boiling water, just like pasta, and drain when it reaches the correct texture.

For the vinaigrette
4 tablespoons rice vinegar
2 tablespoons tamari sauce
2 tablespoons grated peeled fresh ginger
½ teaspoon minced garlic
½ cup extra-virgin olive oil
Sea salt

For the salad
5 cups stemmed and shredded kale
1 cup cooked Israeli couscous
1 cup chopped green beans
1 red bell pepper, diced
½ English cucumber, diced
¼ cup sunflower seeds

To make the vinaigrette:
In a small bowl, whisk together the rice vinegar, tamari sauce, ginger, and garlic.

Whisk in the olive oil until emulsified.

Season with sea salt and set aside.

To make the salad:
In a large bowl, combine the kale, couscous, green beans, red bell pepper, and cucumber with the dressing, and toss until well mixed.

Transfer the salad to a serving bowl, garnish with the sunflower seeds, and serve.

Per Serving Calories: 404; Total Fat: 27g; Sodium: 572mg; Protein: 8g

Kale Caesar Salad

SERVES 4 / PREP: 30 MINUTES / COOK: 0 / TOTAL: 30 MINUTES

Some high-end restaurants will make your Caesar salad tableside in large wooden bowls, creating a theatrical dining experience along with the salad. While ordering a Caesar salad doesn't always have to involve a performance, the dressing still has to have that lovely, salty, freshly made, garlicky bite. One of the most important flavor components in this dressing is the anchovies, so don't omit them.

For the dressing
½ cup mayonnaise
2 anchovies
2 tablespoons freshly squeezed lemon juice
1 teaspoon minced garlic
1 teaspoon Dijon mustard
Water, if needed, to thin the dressing
2 tablespoons grated Parmesan cheese
Sea salt
Freshly ground black pepper

For the salad
6 cups stemmed and chopped kale
4 cooked bacon slices, chopped
½ cup sourdough croutons
¼ cup grated Parmesan cheese plus
    1 tablespoon, divided
1 large hard-boiled egg, grated
4 lemon wedges, for garnish

To make the dressing:
In a blender, blend the mayonnaise, anchovies, lemon juice, garlic, and mustard until very smooth. Thin with the water, if needed.

Transfer the dressing to a small bowl, and stir in the Parmesan.

Season with sea salt and pepper and set aside.

To make the salad:
In a large bowl, toss the kale, bacon, croutons, and ¼ cup of Parmesan with the dressing, until evenly coated.

Divide the salad among 4 plates, and top each with one-fourth of the grated egg and the remaining 1 tablespoon of Parmesan.

Garnish each plate with 1 lemon wedge and serve.

Tip Bacon does not have to be an unhealthy, nitrate-packed product. It can also be completely unprocessed or naturally smoked without any chemicals. Check your local butcher shop for natural bacon, and simply fry it up with a little salt for a nutritious alternative to packaged bacon.

Per Serving Calories: 311; Total Fat: 19g; Sodium: 1,042mg; Protein: 15g

Asian-Inspired Kale & Farfalle Salad

KIDS, LARGE GROUPS, SINGLETONS, MAKE AHEAD

SERVES 4 / PREP: 25 MINUTES / COOK: 15 MINUTES + 30 MINUTES CHILLING / TOTAL: 1 HOUR, 10 MINUTES

Pasta comes in many different shapes—from long noodles to tiny alphabet letters. Farfalle looks like small bowties and is the perfect shape for a pretty, cold salad. The nooks and crannies hold the dressing well, and the distinctive shape shows well when combined with the other ingredients. You can use any type of pasta for this salad; just use a shape big enough to retain its individuality.

For the dressing
½ cup extra-virgin olive oil
¼ cup rice vinegar
2 tablespoons toasted sesame oil
2 tablespoons hoisin sauce
2 tablespoons toasted sesame seeds
1 scallion, minced

For the salad
Pinch sea salt
2½ cups farfalle pasta
4 cups stemmed and shredded kale
2 tomatoes, diced
2 scallions, chopped
½ cup chopped fresh cilantro
½ cup chopped cashews

To make the dressing:
In a small bowl, whisk together the olive oil, rice vinegar, sesame oil, hoisin sauce, sesame seeds, and scallion. Set aside.

To make the salad:
Bring a large pot filled with water and the sea salt to a boil over medium-high heat.

Add the pasta, and cook according to the package instructions until al dente, usually 10 to 12 minutes.

Drain the pasta, and rinse under cold water.

In a large bowl, toss the pasta, kale, tomatoes, scallions, cilantro, and cashews with the dressing until well coated.

Refrigerate for about 30 minutes to develop the flavors, then serve.

Per Serving Calories: 631; Total Fat: 43g; Sodium: 169mg; Protein: 12g

Wilted Kale & Sun-Dried Tomato Salad

VEGANS, PALEOS, GLUTEN-FREES, 30-MINUTE, ONE POT

SERVES 4 / PREP: 15 MINUTES / COOK: 10 MINUTES / TOTAL: 25 MINUTES

The sweet, intense tomato flavor of the sun-dried tomato is exceptional with the slightly bitter taste of fresh kale. This method of preserving tomatoes has been around for centuries. Tomatoes were dried in the sun instead of in ovens to save perishable tomato crops. Today, sun-dried tomatoes can be found packed in oil or dry in bags. If you purchase the dry product, soak the tomatoes in water or oil to reconstitute them before chopping for your recipes.

1 tablespoon extra-virgin olive oil
2 garlic cloves, thinly sliced
1 shallot, minced
8 cups stemmed and coarsely chopped kale
¼ cup white balsamic vinegar
16 oil-packed sun-dried tomatoes, quartered
Sea salt
Freshly ground black pepper

In a large skillet over medium heat, heat the olive oil.

Add the garlic and shallot, and sauté for about 3 minutes, or until fragrant.

Add the kale and toss with tongs for about 3 minutes, or until lightly wilted.

Add the white balsamic vinegar and sun-dried tomatoes, and toss for an additional 3 minutes to warm the tomatoes and wilt the kale.

Season with sea salt and pepper and serve warm.

Tip If you love using sun-dried tomatoes, you can oven-dry your own in large, inexpensive batches. Cut ripe plum tomatoes lengthwise into halves or quarters, and toss them with just enough high-quality olive oil to lightly coat. Scatter the tomatoes in a single layer on parchment-covered baking sheets, and season them lightly with salt and pepper. Dry the tomatoes overnight on the lowest oven temperature possible, and refrigerate the finished product for up to two weeks.

Per Serving Calories: 124; Total Fat: 4g; Sodium: 285mg; Protein: 5g

Massaged Kale Salad
with Lemon Dressing

VEGANS, PALEOS, GLUTEN-FREES, LARGE GROUPS, SINGLETONS, MAKE AHEAD

SERVES 4 / PREP: 15 MINUTES / COOK: 0 MINUTES / TOTAL: 15 MINUTES

Arugula has a sharp, peppery taste that can be surprising if you're not familiar with this lovely green. Try to find tender young arugula leaves if you want less nip to your salad, as their flavor is mellower. Gorgeous radicchio also works beautifully with this salad. The color is a pretty contrast with the deep green kale, and radicchio also has an assertive taste.

1 bunch kale, stemmed, leaves thinly sliced
Juice of 1 lemon
5 tablespoons extra-virgin olive oil
2 tablespoons honey
Sea salt
Freshly ground black pepper
2 cups arugula
1 red chili pepper, thinly sliced into rings
½ sweet onion, thinly sliced
Lemon wedges, for garnish

In a large bowl, using your hands, massage the kale with half the lemon juice and 1 tablespoon of olive oil until the leaves start to soften, about 5 minutes. Set aside.

In a small bowl, whisk together the remaining lemon juice and the honey until blended.

Drizzle the remaining olive oil into the dressing while whisking to emulsify.

Season the dressing with salt and pepper.

Add the dressing, arugula, red chili pepper, and onion and toss to combine.

Arrange the salad on 4 plates, garnish with lemon wedges, and serve.

 Tip Massaging kale with oil creates a softer texture, especially in the larger, tougher leaves. If you're a new kale consumer, this method might make easing into kale simpler.

Per Serving Calories: 212; Total Fat: 18g; Sodium: 108mg; Protein: 4g

Moroccan Kale–Carrot Salad

PALEOS, GLUTEN-FREES, LARGE GROUPS, MAKE AHEAD

SERVES 4 / PREP: 20 MINUTES + 30 MINUTES TO CHILL / COOK: 0 / TOTAL: 50 MINUTES

A humble, inexpensive ingredient, carrots are bursting with flavor and antioxidants such as beta carotene. Carrots are known to support healthy vision and can significantly cut your risk of heart disease. Between the nutrient-rich carrots and the superfood status of kale, this salad should probably be a once-a-week investment in your health.

For the dressing
3 tablespoons apple cider vinegar
1 tablespoon chopped fresh parsley
1 tablespoon chopped fresh cilantro
2 tablespoons honey
2 teaspoons extra-virgin olive oil
1 teaspoon minced garlic
½ teaspoon Dijon mustard
½ teaspoon ground cumin
¼ teaspoon ground coriander
Sea salt
Freshly ground black pepper

For the salad
8 cups stemmed and shredded kale
6 carrots, peeled and shredded

To make the dressing:
In a small bowl, whisk together the cider vinegar, parsley, cilantro, honey, olive oil, garlic, mustard, cumin, and coriander.

Season with sea salt and pepper and set aside.

To make the salad:
In a large bowl, toss together the kale and carrots until well mixed.

Add the dressing and toss to coat.

Refrigerate the salad for at least 30 minutes to mellow the flavors before serving.

Per Serving Calories: 128; Total Fat: 2g; Sodium: 160mg; Protein: 3g

Blueberry-Kale Salad
with Honey-Poppy Seed Dressing

KIDS, GLUTEN-FREES, SINGLETONS, 30-MINUTE

SERVES 4 / PREP: 15 MINUTES / COOK: 0 / TOTAL: 15 MINUTES

Three ingredients, an exceptionally luscious dressing, and on the table in 15 minutes: What's not to love about this beautiful salad? Use an assortment of berries for color and flavor, such as strawberries, blackberries, and raspberries. This dressing works well with most types of fruits and vegetables, so experiment until you get your perfect salad.

For the dressing
¼ cup buttermilk
3 tablespoons honey
2 tablespoons apple cider vinegar
2 teaspoons poppy seeds
Sea salt

For the salad
6 cups stemmed and shredded kale
3 cups fresh blueberries, divided
¼ cup chopped pistachios, divided

To make the dressing:
In a small bowl, whisk together the buttermilk, honey, cider vinegar, and poppy seeds until well blended.

Season with sea salt and set aside.

To make the salad:
In a large bowl, toss the kale with the dressing to coat.

Divide the kale among 4 plates, top each salad with ¾ cup of blueberries and 1 tablespoon of pistachios, and serve.

Tip Blueberries are native to North America and are ranked as having one of the highest amounts of antioxidants of any food. If you want a tart berry, use wild blueberries; if you're looking for a sweeter taste, get cultivated berries from your local store.

Per Serving Calories: 264; Total Fat: 8g; Sodium: 120mg; Protein: 8g

Kale & Roasted Persimmon Salad
with Maple-Walnut Dressing

KIDS, GLUTEN-FREES, LARGE GROUPS, SINGLETONS

SERVES 4 / PREP: 25 MINUTES / COOK: 20 MINUTES + 15 MINUTES TO COOL / TOTAL: 1 HOUR

Crisp fall days, warm snuggly blankets, and rich flavors in food are all hallmarks of autumn. This salad will evoke those memories, even when eaten during other seasons. This dressing might become a family favorite to enjoy with other salads, or as a marinade for meats or poultry. Quality ingredients are important to getting just the right flavor. Use pure maple syrup rather than one cut with high-fructose corn syrup.

For the dressing
¼ cup walnut oil
2 tablespoons apple cider vinegar
2 tablespoons pure maple syrup
1 tablespoon grainy mustard
Sea salt
Freshly ground black pepper

For the salad
2 persimmons, peeled, sliced, and cut into quarters
2 beets, peeled and diced
2 teaspoons extra-virgin olive oil
6 cups stemmed and chopped kale
½ cup slivered almonds

To make the dressing:
In a small bowl, whisk together the walnut oil, cider vinegar, maple syrup, and mustard until well blended.

Season with sea salt and pepper and set aside.

➤

Kale & Roasted Persimmon Salad with Maple-Walnut Dressing, continued

To make the salad:
Preheat the oven to 350°F.

Line a baking sheet with parchment paper.

Spread the persimmons and beets on the prepared baking sheet, and drizzle them with the olive oil. Bake for about 20 minutes, or until softened.

Set aside to cool for 15 minutes.

In a large serving bowl, toss the kale with the dressing until evenly coated.

Top the salad with the roasted persimmons, beets, and slivered almonds.

 Note You can use aluminum foil in place of the parchment paper. Be aware, though, that parchment does not create the browning level that foil does, so there is a chance the food can burn or become too brown.

Per Serving Calories: 255; Total Fat: 13g; Sodium: 159mg; Protein: 8g

Southwest Kale & Black Bean Salad

GLUTEN-FREES, SINGLETONS, 30-MINUTE, MAKE AHEAD

SERVES 4 / PREP: 30 MINUTES / COOK: 0 / TOTAL: 30 MINUTES

When all the ingredients are mixed together and the pale green dressing is drizzled on top, this salad looks like a festive party. The colors are so vibrant and the textures so varied that you might just distract yourself while serving your guests.

For the dressing
½ cup sour cream
½ avocado
½ cup fresh cilantro
1 scallion, chopped
1 garlic clove, quartered
Juice of ½ lime
1 tablespoon honey
Sea salt

For the salad
5 cups stemmed and shredded kale
1 (15-ounce) can sodium-free black beans, drained and rinsed
1 cup fresh corn kernels
1 red bell pepper, diced
1 yellow bell pepper, diced
½ red onion, chopped
½ jalapeño pepper, seeded and finely chopped

To make the dressing:
In a blender, process the sour cream, avocado, cilantro, scallion, garlic, lime juice, and honey until smooth.

Season with sea salt and set aside.

To make the salad:
In a large bowl, toss together the kale, black beans, corn, red bell pepper, yellow bell pepper, red onion, and jalapeño until well mixed.

Transfer to a serving platter, drizzle generously with the dressing, and serve.

Tip Cutting the kernels off the cob doesn't have to be difficult or messy. In a large bowl, simply stand the cob upright and, using a sharp knife, cut the kernels off as close to the cob as possible.

Per Serving Calories: 229; Total Fat: 11g; Sodium: 116mg; Protein: 6g

Wheat Berry–Kale Salad

SERVES 4 / PREP: 25 MINUTES / COOK: 0 / TOTAL: 25 MINUTES

You probably eat wheat berries almost every day and don't even know it. Well, you likely use the processed version of this nutty, wholesome whole grain: whole-wheat flour. Wheat berries are the entire wheat kernel with nothing removed, and are thus incredibly nutritious. You get the endosperm, bran, and germ, which is a great source of fiber, as well as a healthy dose of protein and B vitamins.

For the dressing
½ cup apple juice
½ cup fresh raspberries
3 tablespoons extra-virgin olive oil
2 tablespoons honey
1 tablespoon chopped scallion
1 teaspoon chopped fresh thyme
Sea salt
Freshly ground black pepper

For the salad
2 cups cooked wheat berries
½ English cucumber, diced
1 tablespoon lemon zest
6 cups stemmed and chopped kale
2 cups fresh raspberries
½ cup crumbled goat cheese
1 scallion, thinly sliced on the bias

To make the dressing:
In a blender, blend the apple juice, raspberries, olive oil, honey, scallion, and thyme until smooth.

Season with sea salt and pepper and set aside.

To make the salad:
In a small bowl, toss the wheatberries with half of the dressing until evenly coated.

Stir in the cucumber and lemon zest.

In a medium bowl, toss the kale with the remaining dressing.

Divide the kale among 4 plates. Top each with ½ cup of the wheat berry mixture and ½ cup of raspberries.

Garnish with equal amounts of the goat cheese and scallions and serve.

Tip This sweet, tangy dressing can also be made with high-quality flash-frozen raspberries. Since it's puréed, the perfect texture of fresh raspberries is not as important as the general taste and color in this dressing.

Per Serving Calories: 374; Total Fat: 14g; Sodium: 139mg; Protein: 11g

Kale & Quinoa Salad

GLUTEN-FREES, SINGLETONS, 30-MINUTE

SERVES 4 / PREP: 20 MINUTES / COOK: 0 / TOTAL: 20 MINUTES

Some salads are meant as a starter course to a longer meal, but this one can be a main course for lunch or dinner. If you want a vegan meal, omit the feta cheese or create a more substantial meal with grilled chicken breast or sliced steak on top. This salad mellows nicely in the refrigerator, so double the recipe and enjoy it for two meals.

For the dressing
½ cup extra-virgin olive oil
3 tablespoons balsamic vinegar
1 teaspoon Dijon mustard
2 tablespoons chopped fresh oregano
1 tablespoon chopped fresh basil
Sea salt
Freshly ground black pepper

For the salad
4 cups finely chopped kale, stemmed, thoroughly washed, and dried
2 cups cooked quinoa
1 tomato, chopped
1 green bell pepper, diced
½ red onion, chopped
½ English cucumber, diced
½ cup crumbled feta cheese

To make the dressing:
In a small bowl, whisk together the olive oil, balsamic vinegar, Dijon mustard, oregano, and basil until combined.

Season with sea salt and pepper and set aside.

To make the salad:
In a large bowl, toss together the kale, quinoa, tomatoes, bell pepper, onion, and cucumber.

Add the dressing and toss until well mixed.

Top with the feta and serve.

Tip Have you ever rinsed quinoa and noticed a white foam on the water? This foam is the saponins found on the outside of the quinoa, and it causes this seed to be bitter and soapy tasting. Saponins might be toxic to the body, so don't skip the rinsing step when preparing quinoa.

Per Serving Calories: 471; Total Fat: 31g; Sodium: 267mg; Protein: 11g

8

Hand-Helds

Kale & Goat Cheese Sandwiches

SERVES 2 / PREP: 15 MINUTES / COOK: 10 MINUTES / TOTAL: 25 MINUTES

This is not your standard grilled cheese sandwich. Golden, crunchy bread, tangy cheese, sweet tomatoes, and earthy beets combine in this culinary masterpiece that needs no additional embellishment. Don't substitute butter for the olive oil to brush the bread; the resulting taste and texture would not be the same. Try a sun-dried tomato–infused oil for a double flavor kick. You can find it at specialty food stores.

4 slices French-style baguette, cut ½-inch thick on the bias
2 tablespoons extra-virgin olive oil, divided
4 ounces goat cheese, divided
2 cups stemmed and finely chopped kale
1 tomato, seeded and diced
2 cooked beets, peeled and diced
Sea salt
Freshly ground black pepper

Brush both sides of each bread slice with the olive oil. Place a large skillet over medium-high heat.

When the skillet is hot, add the bread, pressing down with the flat of a spatula.

Cook for about 2 minutes. Check the bottom and flip when the bread is golden brown.

Repeat with the other side of the bread until golden, about 2 minutes. Place the bread on a cutting board.

In a small bowl, stir together the goat cheese and kale until well blended. Spread 2 slices of bread with half of the goat cheese-kale mixture each.

Evenly divide and layer the tomato and beets on top of the goat cheese-kale mixture. Close each sandwich with the other 2 slices of bread and serve warm.

Tip Unpasteurized cheeses, such as goat cheese, can contain a bacterium called listeria that can be harmful, especially if you're pregnant. If you are pregnant, substitute a soft pasteurized cheese that is labeled as containing no raw milk.

Per Serving Calories: 644; Total Fat: 36g; Sodium: 837mg; Protein: 29g

Kale–Sweet Potato Toasts

KIDS

SERVES 4 / PREP: 15 MINUTES / COOK: 40 MINUTES / TOTAL: 55 MINUTES

Crostini are convenient snacks that feature a variety of toppings on lightly toasted slices of crusty bread. Sweet potato and kale make a robust choice for times when you want a more substantial snack or a light lunch. Dice the sweet potatoes small enough so they cook quickly and stay on the bread easily.

2 sweet potatoes, cut into ¼-inch dice
½ cup extra-virgin olive oil, divided
2 teaspoons minced garlic
8 cups stemmed and chopped kale
Sea salt
Freshly ground black pepper
1 baguette, cut into 3-inch-long pieces, about ¼-inch thick
1 cup shaved Asiago cheese, divided
¼ cup chopped fresh basil, divided

Preheat the oven to 350°F.

Line a baking sheet with parchment paper.

In a medium bowl, toss the sweet potato pieces with 1 tablespoon of olive oil. Spread them on the prepared baking sheet.

Bake for about 30 minutes, or until lightly browned and tender.

Transfer the potatoes to a bowl to cool.

Increase the oven temperature to broil.

In a large skillet over medium heat, heat 4 tablespoons of olive oil.

Add the garlic and sauté for about 2 minutes, or until fragrant.

Add the kale. Using tongs, toss for about 6 minutes, or until wilted and tender.

Remove the skillet from the heat, and season with sea salt and pepper.

Brush the baguette slices with the remaining 3 tablespoons of olive oil and place them on a baking sheet. Broil for about 1 minute, or until golden and crispy. Remove the sheet from the oven and turn the bread over.

⟶

Mound equal amounts of the wilted kale on each slice, top with equal amounts of the sweet potato mixture, and sprinkle equal amounts of the Asiago on top.

Return the sheet to the oven and broil for about 30 seconds, or until the cheese melts.

Garnish with the basil and serve.

Note You can use aluminum foil in place of the parchment paper. Be aware, though, that parchment does not create the browning level that foil does, so there is a chance the food can burn or become too brown.

Tip Hard cheeses become firmer and more pungent as they age, and the different choices offer unique taste and texture benefits to your cooking. Asiago has a sweeter flavor than Parmesan and is produced traditionally in the Alpine region of northeastern Italy. Superior Asiago is aged about nine months.

Per Serving (2 pieces) Calories: 298; Total Fat: 17g; Sodium: 372mg; Protein: 9g

Simple Kale-Mozzarella Sandwiches

KIDS, LARGE GROUPS, SINGLETONS, 30-MINUTE

SERVES 4 / PREP: 15 MINUTES / COOK: 5 MINUTES / TOTAL: 20 MINUTES

Mozzarella is sometimes known as a tasteless, good-melting cheese mostly found on pizzas. This cheese is traditionally produced from buffalo's milk and created using a method called *pasta filata*. The cheese is spun from the milk and cut. If you can find a true fresh mozzarella cheese, the flavor of this sandwich will be sublime.

8 slices crusty Italian bread
¼ cup basil pesto, divided
16 oil-packed sun-dried tomatoes, divided
6 ounces fresh mozzarella cheese, thinly sliced, divided
4 cups Blanched Kale (page 33), divided
Freshly ground black pepper

Preheat the oven to broil.

Place the bread slices on a baking sheet, and put them under the broiler for about 30 seconds, or until lightly toasted.

Spread each piece with 1½ teaspoons of pesto.

Top 4 bread slices with 4 sun-dried tomatoes each. Then top each with an equal amount of mozzarella cheese.

Divide the Blanched Kale among the 4 sandwiches and season with pepper.

Top each sandwich with 1 of the 4 remaining bread slices, cut on a diagonal, and serve.

Tip Making your own mozzarella cheese, if you are feeling adventurous, can be done in as little as two hours, depending on your technique. The best ingredients to use are whole milk, rennet, citric acid, and some salt. The finished cheese is creamy, tastes incredibly fresh, and is quite possibly addictive.

Per Serving Calories: 336; Total Fat: 10g; Sodium: 835mg; Protein: 21g

Fresh Kale & Cucumber Sandwiches

KIDS, SINGLETONS, 30-MINUTE

SERVES 4 / PREP: 30 MINUTES / COOK: 0 / TOTAL: 30 MINUTES

Cucumber sandwiches are a staple of traditional high teas or formal luncheons. These delicate creations are usually cut into little shapes such as stars, hearts, and circles. However, you won't be cutting this sizable sandwich into shapes—and depending on the amount of kale, it might be difficult to even take a bite! Cucumber adds a cool crispness to the mix of ingredients—and don't skimp on the mustard. Its earthy flavor is crucial to the success of this dish.

3 cups stemmed and chopped kale
1 teaspoon extra-virgin olive oil
1 tablespoon freshly squeezed lemon juice
8 slices whole-grain bread
¼ cup grainy mustard, divided
1 English cucumber, thinly sliced
Sea salt
1 tablespoon chopped fresh dill

In a large bowl, using your hands, massage the kale in the olive oil and lemon juice until well coated. Set aside for 15 minutes.

Toast the bread and spread each piece with 1½ teaspoons of mustard.

Top 4 pieces of bread generously with equal amounts of cucumber in 2 layers.

Lightly salt the cucumber, and sprinkle each sandwich evenly with dill.

Generously mound each sandwich with an equal amount of kale, top each with 1 of the 4 remaining bread slices, and serve immediately.

Tip **You might not know that the familiar mustard in your refrigerator is** created from whole mustard seeds mixed with other ingredients and then puréed or crushed into a smooth condiment. Grainy mustard uses whole, or partially crushed, seeds that create a different flavor. This sandwich is best with the grainy product.

Per Serving Calories: 252; Total Fat: 5g; Sodium: 552mg; Protein: 12g

Kale & Bean Tacos

SERVES 2 / PREP: 30 MINUTES / COOK: 0 / TOTAL: 30 MINUTES

Kids love tacos. They enjoy putting them together as well as the messy crunchiness of eating them. So why not pile your tacos with nutritious kale and watch your kids scarf it down without protest? This recipe produces a vegetarian taco, but you can add seasoned ground beef or chopped chicken.

1 (15-ounce) can black beans, drained and rinsed

1 tomato, chopped

1 scallion, chopped

½ jalapeño pepper, minced

1 teaspoon chili powder

½ teaspoon ground cumin

4 large kale leaves, stemmed

½ avocado, sliced

¼ cup sour cream, divided

2 tablespoons chopped fresh cilantro, divided

In a medium bowl, using a fork, mash the black beans.

Add the tomato, scallion, jalapeño pepper, chili powder, and cumin, and mix well.

Lay the kale leaves on a flat surface, and spoon the bean mixture, evenly divided, into the middle of each leaf. Top each with equal amounts of avocado, sour cream, and cilantro.

Fold the leaves up and around the filling to form wraps.

Serve two per person.

Tip The sour cream can be omitted to create a vegan meal or substituted with a soy product, even plain soy yogurt. The snowy white color is lovely for presentation, and the tangy sour taste complements the rest of the ingredients.

Per Serving (2 tacos) Calories: 536; Total Fat: 19g; Sodium: 96mg; Protein: 25g

Kale Croquettes

SERVES 4 / PREP: 30 MINUTES / COOK: 30 MINUTES / TOTAL: 1 HOUR

Croquettes are small balls, or patties, of vegetables, meats, and herbs that are breaded and fried to a crispy golden brown. The filling can be just about anything, as long as it holds its shape firmly like this tasty kale creation. Try dipping these croquettes in hot mustard or picalilli, a condiment made from chopped pickled vegetables and spices.

8 cups water

2 pounds kale, stemmed

1 sweet onion, finely chopped

2 eggs, lightly beaten, plus additional for shaping (if needed)

¾ cup grated Swiss cheese

¾ cup bread crumbs, plus additional for shaping

½ teaspoon smoked paprika

Sea salt

Freshly ground black pepper

¼ cup extra-virgin olive oil, divided

In a large pot over medium-high heat, bring the water and kale to a boil.

Boil for about 10 minutes, or until tender.

Drain the kale, squeezing out as much water as possible.

Chop the kale finely, and transfer it to a large bowl.

Add the onion, eggs, Swiss cheese, bread crumbs, and paprika to the chopped kale, and stir to mix well.

Season with sea salt and pepper.

If needed, adjust the texture of the mixture with more egg or bread crumbs so it holds together well. Using your hands, shape the mixture into 12 small, egg-shaped cakes.

In a large skillet over medium-high heat, fry 2 tablespoons of olive oil and 6 croquettes for 5 minutes and turn. Fry for about 5 minutes more, or until golden brown. Transfer to a plate.

Repeat with the remaining 2 tablespoons of olive oil and 6 croquettes and serve.

Per Serving (3 croquettes) Calories: 425; Total Fat: 22g; Sodium: 379mg; Protein: 18g

Crunchy Kale Coleslaw Wraps

KIDS, VEGANS, 30-MINUTE, MAKE AHEAD

SERVES 6 / PREP: 30 MINUTES / COOK: 0 / TOTAL: 30 MINUTES

The crunch in this slaw comes partially from the jicama. If you're unfamiliar with this vegetable, this recipe is a great way to discover what a wonderful addition it can be to your kitchen. Once you peel off the tough brown skin, jicama has a refreshing, crisp, juicy interior similar to a pear. Jicama is almost fat free and low in sodium and calories as well as high in fiber, vitamin C, and iron. You can use any leftovers shredded in wraps, diced for salads, and sliced as a crunchy snack.

6 cups stemmed and shredded kale
1 cup shredded carrot
½ jicama, shredded
1 red bell pepper, thinly sliced
1 yellow bell pepper, thinly sliced
2 scallions, julienned
½ cup chopped fresh cilantro
Juice of 1 lime
2 tablespoons extra-virgin olive oil
Sea salt
Freshly ground black pepper
6 (8-inch) brown rice tortillas, warmed in the microwave or oven
¼ cup hummus, divided

In a large bowl, toss together the kale, carrot, jicama, red bell pepper, yellow bell pepper, scallions, cilantro, lime juice, and olive oil until well mixed.

Season with sea salt and pepper.

Lay the tortillas on a clean work surface, and spread 2 teaspoons of hummus across the middle of each.

Divide the kale mixture among the tortillas, tightly fold them into wraps, and serve.

Tip Cilantro has a strong taste that is repellent to some people and a favorite recipe addition for others. Cilantro can help detox the body of metals, lower blood cholesterol levels, and cut the risk of many diseases such as cancer, diabetes, and heart disease.

Per Serving Calories: 263; Total Fat: 8g; Sodium: 281mg; Protein: 6g

Kale & Turkey Roll-Ups

KIDS, MEAT LOVERS, GLUTEN-FREES, SINGLETONS, 30-MINUTE

SERVES 4 / PREP: 30 MINUTES / COOK: 0 / TOTAL: 30 MINUTES

Kale stands in for traditional tortillas in this simple wrap, so use leaves large and tender enough to roll up. Avoid using the tougher outer leaves, and slice out the stems to avoid any unpleasant texture. This wrap can be made with any type of meat, but turkey tastes incredible with salty bacon, creamy avocado, and tangy blue cheese. Your chosen deli meat should be a natural product with no added nitrates or salt for best results.

4 large kale leaves, stemmed

8 slices low-sodium oven-roasted turkey breast

4 cooked bacon slices

2 tomatoes, sliced

1 avocado, thinly sliced

½ cup blue cheese crumbles, divided

Spread the kale leaves out on a clean work surface.

Place 2 turkey slices on each leaf, and top each with 1 bacon slice.

Layer on the tomato and avocado slices in equal amounts, and sprinkle each with about 2 tablespoons of blue cheese apiece.

Fold the leaves up to form packages and serve 1 per person.

Tip **Leftover turkey meat can be used in this wrap instead of deli meat. Either slice the turkey very thinly, or shred it so you can wrap the kale leaves tightly and smoothly around it.**

Per Serving (1 wrap) Calories: 304; Total Fat: 22g; Sodium: 907mg; Protein: 17g

Kale–Pesto Veggie Pizza

KIDS, LARGE GROUPS, SINGLETONS

SERVES 4 / PREP: 25 MINUTES / COOK: 20 MINUTES / TOTAL: 45 MINUTES

Did you know you can make pesto out of pretty much any herb, green, nut, and oil, depending on the taste you want and the recipe? You'll have leftover pesto after you make these savory pizzas, so refrigerate the remainder in a sealed container for up to 2 weeks. Use the pesto to make other pizzas or for pasta, dips, or a sandwich spread.

For the pesto
4 cups chopped Blanched Kale (page 33)
1 cup fresh basil leaves
½ cup pine nuts
½ cup grated Asiago cheese
2 garlic cloves
½ cup extra virgin olive oil
Sea salt
Freshly ground black pepper

For the pizza
All-purpose flour, for dusting
Pizza dough for 1 (10-inch) pizza, either premade or homemade
8 oil-packed sun-dried tomatoes, chopped
½ cup sliced mushrooms
½ green pepper, chopped
½ red onion, thinly sliced
½ cup grated Parmesan cheese
1 cup shredded mozzarella cheese

To make the pesto:
In a food processor, pulse the Blanched Kale, basil, pine nuts, Asiago, garlic, and olive oil until well blended and smooth.

Transfer the pesto to a bowl, and season with sea salt and pepper.

To make the pizza:
Preheat the oven to 400°F. Dust a clean work surface with flour, and roll out the pizza dough in a circle so it is about 12 inches in diameter.

Place the pizza dough on a baking sheet lined with parchment, and spread a generous amount of pesto on the dough, leaving about 1½ inches of dough on the outside edge.

Top the pizza with the sun-dried tomatoes, mushrooms, green pepper, red onion, and Parmesan. Sprinkle the mozzarella cheese over the pizza.

Fold the edges of the pizza over toward the center in an overlapping pattern about 1-inch wide, pressing so that the dough sticks together.

Bake the pizza in the preheated oven for about 20 minutes, or until golden and crispy and the cheese melts. Cut into 8 slices and serve 2 per person.

Per Serving (2 pieces) Calories: 489; Total Fat: 31g; Sodium: 854mg; Protein: 25g

Kale—Chicken Pizza

KIDS, MEAT LOVERS, SINGLETONS

SERVES 4 / PREP: 15 MINUTES / COOK: 20 MINUTES / TOTAL: 35 MINUTES

Pizza is one of the most popular meal choices because it is delicious, and there is something fun about laying out all the toppings and then holding cheesy pieces in your hand to eat. Premade pizza crusts make this whole process incredibly simple. You can even prepare your pizzas in advance to save time. If you want to make your pizza crust dough from scratch, follow the usual instructions for proofing, forming, and baking.

1 (10-inch) premade pizza crust

Extra-virgin olive oil, for brushing

2 tomatoes, thinly sliced, or 1 cup prepared pizza sauce

3 cups chopped Blanched Kale (page 33)

1 cooked boneless, skinless chicken breast, chopped

1 tablespoon fresh oregano

1 cup shredded part-skim mozzarella cheese

1 teaspoon red pepper flakes (optional)

Preheat the oven to 400°F.

Put the pizza crust on a baking sheet, and brush the edges with the olive oil.

Layer on the tomatoes, leaving about ½ inch of bare crust around the edges.

Spread the Blanched Kale and the chicken over the tomatoes, and sprinkle with the oregano.

Top with the mozzarella cheese, and sprinkle on the red pepper flakes (if using).

Bake the pizza in the preheated oven for 15 to 20 minutes, or until the crust is golden and crispy and the cheese is melted and bubbly.

Cut into 8 slices and serve 2 per person.

Tip Premade pizza crust is often packaged with a packet of pizza sauce. It is better to make your own sauce, or top the crust with a generous layer of pesto or fresh vegetables, than to use the packaged sauce, as it's often extremely high in salt and sugar.

Per Serving (2 pieces) Calories: 283; Total Fat: 10g; Sodium: 655mg; Protein: 26g

Chickpea, Kale & Rice Burgers

KIDS, LARGE GROUPS, SINGLETONS, MAKE AHEAD

SERVES 5 / PREP: 20 MINUTES / COOK: 25 MINUTES / TOTAL: 45 MINUTES

This recipe doubles easily and freezes well, so make a huge batch for handy meals and snacks right out of the freezer. Cook the patties completely, and cool them before placing in individual sandwich zip-top bags and freezing. If you want something more exotic than a standard bun, try these burgers stuffed into pita bread topped with a tangy Greek *tzatziki* (garlic, yogurt, cucumber) sauce.

1 (15-ounce) can chickpeas, drained and rinsed
1½ cups chopped Blanched Kale (page 33)
¾ cup cooked basmati rice
1 scallion, chopped
2 tablespoons quick-cooking oats
2 tablespoons finely chopped oil-packed sun-dried tomatoes
2 tablespoons chopped fresh basil
1 tablespoon chopped fresh oregano
1 garlic clove, coarsely chopped
1½ teaspoons extra virgin olive oil
1 large egg
Sea salt
Freshly ground black pepper
Hamburger buns, for serving (optional)

Preheat the oven to 350°F. Line a baking sheet with parchment paper and set aside.

In a food processor, pulse the chickpeas, blanched kale, rice, scallion, oats, sundried tomatoes, basil, oregano, and garlic to coarsely chop. Transfer the mixture to a large bowl. Add the olive oil and egg.

Using your hands, mix all the ingredients together until you can form patties. Season with sea salt and pepper.

Shape the mixture into 5 (3-inch) patties, and place them on the prepared sheet.

Bake the patties in the preheated oven for about 15 minutes, or until lightly golden on top. Flip them and bake for an additional 10 minutes.

Serve on hamburger buns (if using) with traditional burger toppings, or plain as a tasty snack.

Tip **Oats are not considered gluten-free, as they are usually processed in plants that also manufacture products using other grains and can be cross-contaminated. If you want gluten-free burgers, use certified gluten-free oats.**

Per Serving Calories: 212; Total Fat: 4g; Sodium: 106mg; Protein: 10g

Kale & Egg Salad Sandwiches

SERVES 4 / PREP: 30 MINUTES / COOK: 0 / TOTAL: 30 MINUTES

Good egg salad is a culinary aspiration for many, and the exact ingredients and amounts are the stuff of legends in many church groups and cooking competitions. This simple recipe features tangy pickles, a touch of spicy Dijon mustard, and a generous handful of shredded kale for color and flavor. If you have a favorite egg salad recipe you've perfected over the years, add the shredded kale to that and enjoy the additional health benefits.

2 cups stemmed and finely chopped kale
1 teaspoon extra-virgin olive oil
6 hard-boiled eggs, peeled
½ cup mayonnaise
1 teaspoon Dijon mustard
¼ cup chopped dill pickle
1 scallion, chopped
Sea salt
Freshly ground black pepper
4 English muffins, split
Paprika, for garnish

In a large bowl, using your hands, massage the kale leaves in the olive oil until evenly coated. Set aside to tenderize for 15 minutes.

Grate the eggs into the kale; add the mayonnaise, mustard, pickle, and scallion, and stir to combine.

Season with sea salt and pepper.

Toast the English muffins, top each half with a generous scoop of the kale-egg salad, and sprinkle with paprika.

Serve open faced.

Refrigerate any extra egg salad in a sealed container up to 3 days.

Tip Have you ever peeled a hard-boiled egg and ended up with the shell sticking to it and chunks of white removed? This is because the eggs are fresh, and the membranes surrounding the white have not had a chance to shrink away from the shell. Keep the eggs in the refrigerator for at least one week before boiling them, and the shells will come off cleanly.

Per Serving (2 halves) Calories: 381; Total Fat: 20g; Sodium: 761mg; Protein: 16g

Kale-Black Bean Quesadillas

KIDS, LARGE GROUPS, SINGLETONS, MAKE AHEAD

SERVES 4 / PREP: 30 MINUTES / COOK: 10 MINUTES / TOTAL: 40 MINUTES

You do not need a barbecue to produce these crunchy, cheesy beauties, although the lightly charred taste from grilling is outstanding. Without a barbecue, or in inclement weather, arrange the finished quesadillas on a baking sheet and put them under the broiler for about two minutes per side. You can assemble the quesadillas ahead of time and leave them covered in the refrigerator until you're ready to serve them—just bring them to room temperature before finishing on the grill or under the broiler.

1 (15-ounce) can black beans, drained and rinsed
1 teaspoon chili powder
½ jalapeño pepper, minced
4 (10-inch) whole-wheat tortillas
Cooking spray
2 scallions, chopped, divided
1 large tomato, chopped, divided
3 cups stemmed and shredded kale
1 cup Monterey Jack cheese, divided
¼ cup sour cream
¼ cup chopped fresh cilantro

Preheat the grill to medium.

In a medium bowl, using a fork, coarsely mash the black beans.

Add the chili powder and jalapeño, and stir to combine.

Spray 2 tortillas with cooking spray, and place them oil-side down on a cutting board.

Spoon half of the bean mixture onto each tortilla, spreading it to the edges.

Sprinkle half of the scallion and half of the tomatoes over each.

Spread 1½ cups of kale evenly over each tortilla, and top each with ½ cup of cheese.

Cover each filled tortilla with 1 of the 2 remaining tortillas, pressing firmly in place, and coat lightly with cooking spray.

Place the quesadillas on the grill, and cook for about 10 minutes, or until the quesadilla is lightly charred and crispy and the cheese is melted, turning once.

Cut the quesadillas into quarters, and serve with the sour cream and cilantro.

Per Serving Calories: 381; Total Fat: 14g; Sodium: 334mg; Protein: 20g

Kale, Quinoa & Lettuce Tacos

KIDS, VEGANS, GLUTEN-FREES, SINGLETONS, 30-MINUTE

SERVES 4 / PREP: 30 MINUTES / COOK: 0 / TOTAL: 30 MINUTES

Fresh, crispy lettuce leaves are perfect to wrap savory fillings—they're easy to fold and add very little taste or calories to the finished dish. This recipe uses tender Boston lettuce leaves, but romaine would also work well—or even kale, if you want to double up on your kale portions. Any non-iceberg lettuce is quite high in vitamins C and K, phytonutrients, and fiber—so it isn't the nutritional lightweight it may seem.

3 cups stemmed and finely shredded kale
1 cup cooked quinoa
½ red bell pepper, finely chopped
1 cup shredded carrot
2 celery stalks, minced
2 tablespoons chopped fresh chives
2 tablespoons freshly squeezed lemon juice
1 tablespoon extra-virgin olive oil
Sea salt
Freshly ground black pepper
8 Boston lettuce leaves

In a large bowl, mix together the kale, quinoa, red bell pepper, carrot, celery, chives, lemon juice, and olive oil.

Season with sea salt and pepper.

Scoop equal amounts of the kale mixture into each lettuce leaf and fold like a taco.

Serve 2 per person.

Per Serving (2 tacos) Calories: 163; Total Fat: 5g; Sodium: 115mg; Protein: 5g

Kale, Bacon & Tomato Sandwiches

KIDS, MEAT LOVERS, SINGLETONS, 30-MINUTE

SERVES 2 / PREP: 20 MINUTES / COOK: 0 / TOTAL: 20 MINUTES

BLTs are a classic diner sandwich. Some could argue that the tomato and bacon are really the most important parts of the sandwich—so swapping the lettuce for kale should not garner too much protest, even from BLT fanatics. Kale is more flavorful than regular iceberg lettuce and adds a lovely complexity to this simple sandwich, along with the peameal bacon.

3 tablespoons mayonnaise
1 tablespoon basil pesto
4 slices sourdough bread
4 cooked peameal bacon slices
1 beefsteak tomato, cut into ¼-inch-thick slices
3 cups stemmed and shredded kale
Sea salt
Freshly ground black pepper

In a small bowl, whisk together the mayonnaise and pesto.

Toast the bread slices, and place them on a clean work surface.

Spread 1 tablespoon of the basil mayonnaise onto each slice.

On 2 pieces of bread, layer 2 slices of bacon, half of the tomato slices, and 1½ cups of kale.

Top each sandwich with a second slice of bread, cut the sandwiches in half, and serve.

Per Serving Calories: 487; Total Fat: 14g; Sodium: 1,803mg; Protein: 31g

9

Main Dishes

Roasted Tofu & Squash with Kale

GLUTEN-FREES, LARGE GROUPS, SINGLETONS

SERVES 4 / PREP: 25 MINUTES + 2 HOURS TO MARINATE / COOK: 45 MINUTES / TOTAL: 3 HOURS, 10 MINUTES

Butternut squash is usually treated as a vegetable in recipes, but it is technically a fruit because of its seeds. Squash is very low in fat and high in fiber and potassium. This tasty recipe combines all the goodness of squash with cancer-fighting and heart-friendly tofu, creating a very healthy meal for your family.

3 tablespoons balsamic vinegar
2 tablespoons tamari sauce
1 tablespoon honey
¼ teaspoon sea salt, plus 1 pinch, divided
Pinch freshly ground black pepper
1 (14-ounce) block extra-firm tofu, washed, drained, and cut into ½-inch cubes
1 (2 pound) butternut squash, peeled, seeded, and cut into ½-inch chunks
¼ cup extra-virgin olive oil, divided
½ teaspoon ground cinnamon
6 cups stemmed and chopped kale
¼ cup cilantro leaves
½ cup pumpkin seeds

In a small bowl, stir together the vinegar, tamari sauce, honey, salt, and pepper until well blended.

In a medium bowl, pour the vinegar mixture over the tofu cubes. Toss to coat, cover the bowl with plastic wrap, and refrigerate for 2 hours to marinate.

Preheat the oven to 375°F and line a baking sheet with parchment paper.

Remove the bowl from the refrigerator, and add the butternut squash, 2 tablespoons olive oil, and cinnamon. Mix well and spread the mixture onto the baking sheet.

Roast the tofu and squash, turning once, until golden and tender, about 35 minutes. Set aside.

In a large skillet over medium-high heat, heat the remaining 2 tablespoons of olive oil.

Add the kale and begin tossing with tongs. As the kale wilts, continue tossing to move any raw kale to the heat.

When all the kale is wilted and tender, after about 10 minutes, season with the additional sea salt.

Add the tofu, squash, and cilantro to the kale and toss to combine.

Divide the kale mixture between 4 plates, top with pumpkin seeds, and serve.

Tip For a slightly heartier version of this dish, serve it over a bed of your favorite grain, such as quinoa, brown rice, or farro.

Per Serving Calories: 470; Total Fat: 25g; Sodium: 732mg; Protein: 21g

Kale—Stuffed Tomatoes

KIDS, GLUTEN-FREES, LARGE GROUPS

SERVES 4 / PREP: 35 MINUTES / COOK: 50 MINUTES / TOTAL: 1 HOUR, 25 MINUTES

Tomatoes make handy, delicious containers for an assortment of tempting fillings, including this savory kale mixture. Don't skip step 4, which purges some liquid from the tomatoes, or your stuffed vegetables could end up a wilted mess. If you're looking for a unique appetizer, make this filling and spoon it into cherry tomatoes instead of full-size ones. This takes some work, but the results are worth it.

Cooking spray
8 large, firm, ripe tomatoes
Sea salt
2 teaspoons extra-virgin olive oil
1 sweet onion, finely chopped
2 teaspoons minced garlic
6 cups chopped Blanched Kale (page 33)
2 tablespoons balsamic vinegar
1 cup cooked lentils, rinsed and drained
¼ cup chopped fresh basil
Freshly ground black pepper
1 cup crumbled feta cheese, divided

Preheat the oven to 350°F.

Lightly coat a large baking dish with cooking spray.

Slice the tops off the tomatoes, and carefully scoop out the insides, leaving the shells intact. Reserve the pulp.

Sprinkle the tomato shells with sea salt, and place them upside down on paper towels to drain for 30 minutes.

In a large skillet over medium-high heat, heat the olive oil.

Add the onion and garlic, and sauté for about 3 minutes, or until translucent.

Add the Blanched Kale. Using tongs, toss for about 6 minutes, or until wilted and tender.

Stir in the reserved tomato pulp and balsamic vinegar. Cook, stirring occasionally, for 10 minutes. Remove from the heat.

Stir in the lentils and basil, and season with the pepper.

Place the tomato shells in the prepared baking dish, and spoon equal amounts of the filling into each.

Top each with an equal amount of the feta.

Bake for about 30 minutes, or until the tomatoes are tender, and serve.

Tip **Finding fresh basil can sometimes be impossible, so buy extra bunches when you see quality herbs at the store or market. Purée the herb in a food processor, and freeze the purée in ice cube trays for when you need a basil boost in your dishes. Simply drop the frozen basil cubes into your soups and stews.**

Per Serving (2 tomatoes) Calories: 423; Total Fat: 12g; Sodium: 542mg; Protein: 25g

Creamy Kale–Pesto Penne

KIDS, VEGANS, LARGE GROUPS, SINGLETONS, 30-MINUTE

SERVES 4 / PREP: 10 MINUTES / COOK: 20 MINUTES / TOTAL: 30 MINUTES

Using pesto in pasta is a clever method of getting lots of nutrients and taste without spending hours over a hot stove. Don't leave out the avocado in this pesto; it creates a luscious texture. Peel the avocado with your hands rather than slicing away the tough skin with a knife. The highest concentration of carotenoids in avocados is in the flesh just below the skin.

4 cups whole-grain penne

4 cups stemmed and coarsely chopped kale

½ cup fresh basil leaves, plus additional for garnish

½ avocado, cut into chunks

3 garlic cloves

¼ cup pine nuts

2 tablespoons extra-virgin olive oil

1 tablespoon freshly squeezed lemon juice

¼ cup water, or as needed

Sea salt

Freshly ground black pepper

In a large pot, cook the pasta according to the package instructions. Drain and set aside.

While the pasta cooks, add the kale, basil, avocado, garlic, pine nuts, olive oil, and lemon juice to a food processor, and pulse until coarsely chopped.

Scrape down the sides of the processor. Turn it back on and pour in the water, while blending, until the pesto is a thick, creamy texture. Use as much water as needed for the desired texture.

Season the pesto with sea salt and pepper and set aside.

Toss the hot pasta with as much pesto as you like, or until the penne is well coated. If you have leftover pesto, refrigerate it in a sealed container for up to 1 week.

Serve the pasta garnished with the basil leaves.

Tip **This pasta is quite easy to modify if you need a gluten-free or vegan alternative. Simply swap out the whole-grain penne for brown rice pasta or another gluten-free alternative.**

Per Serving Calories: 551; Total Fat: 19g; Sodium: 25mg; Protein: 15g

Kale—Stuffed Squash Boats

KIDS, PALEOS, GLUTEN-FREES, LARGE GROUPS, MAKE AHEAD

SERVES 4 / PREP: 15 MINUTES / COOK: 40 MINUTES / TOTAL: 55 MINUTES

If you're pressed for time but still want this gorgeous dish on a busy evening, assemble the entire recipe the night before or earlier in the day. Simply refrigerate the filled squash, then transfer them to the oven to heat, covered, for a quick 20 minutes. You can also make the filling and use it to stuff other vegetables like zucchini, red bell peppers, or hollowed-out sweet potatoes.

2 acorn squash, halved and seeded
2 teaspoons extra-virgin olive oil, divided
1 teaspoon butter
½ sweet onion, chopped
1 teaspoon minced garlic
1 teaspoon ground cumin
½ teaspoon ground coriander
½ teaspoon ground cinnamon
3 cups shredded Blanched Kale (page 33)
1 cup cooked quinoa
¼ cup chopped pistachios
Sea salt
Freshly ground black pepper

Preheat the oven to 450°F.

On a baking sheet, place the acorn squash cut-side down. Brush the outsides of each with 1 teaspoon of olive oil.

Bake the squash for about 30 minutes, or until tender but not deflated.

Remove the squash from the oven. Turn them hollow-side up, and cover tightly with foil to keep warm. Set aside.

In a large skillet over medium-high heat, melt the butter and sauté the onion and garlic for about 3 minutes, or until softened.

Stir in the cumin, coriander, and cinnamon, and sauté for about 2 minutes, or until the spices become fragrant.

Add the Blanched Kale and quinoa, and cook for 5 minutes, stirring frequently.

Remove from the heat, stir in the pistachios, and season with sea salt and pepper.

Spoon one-fourth of the kale mixture into each acorn half.

Serve one-half squash per person.

Per Serving Calories: 267; Total Fat: 8g; Sodium: 96mg; Protein: 8g

Kale Mac & Cheese

KIDS, LARGE GROUPS, MAKE AHEAD

SERVES 8 / PREP: 20 MINUTES / COOK: 40 MINUTES / TOTAL: 1 HOUR

Homemade mac and cheese does not have the signature glow-in-the-dark orange sauce of packaged mixes, and the flavor is not sharp but delightfully creamy and smooth. You might enjoy the convenience of a mix-and-stir pasta dish, but if you make this delectable casserole the day before, it's just as simple—and much more nutritious—to just bake it right from the refrigerator.

4 cups whole-wheat elbow macaroni
1 cup evaporated milk
½ cup milk
1 cup Cheddar cheese
1 cup Gruyère cheese
1 teaspoon ground nutmeg
Pinch cayenne pepper
Pinch sea salt
Freshly ground black pepper
4 cups chopped Blanched Kale (page 33)
½ cup bread crumbs
1 teaspoon melted butter

Preheat the oven to 350°F.

Cook the pasta according to the package instructions. Drain and transfer to a large bowl.

In a large saucepan set over medium heat, bring the evaporated milk and milk to a simmer.

Whisk in the Cheddar and Gruyère, and continue whisking for 1 to 2 minutes, or until melted.

Whisk in the nutmeg and cayenne pepper.

Season with sea salt and pepper.

Add the cheese sauce and Blanched Kale to the pasta, and stir until well mixed.

Spoon the macaroni into a large 3-quart baking dish.

In a small bowl, stir together the bread crumbs and butter. Top the casserole with the crumbs.

Bake for about 40 minutes, or until bubbly and lightly browned, and serve.

Per Serving Calories: 460; Total Fat: 21g; Sodium: 487mg; Protein: 23g

Kale—Salmon Packets

KIDS, GLUTEN-FREES, SINGLETONS, MAKE AHEAD

SERVES 4 / PREP: 25 MINUTES / COOK: 15 MINUTES / TOTAL: 40 MINUTES

This cooking technique steams the fish and kale in the fish's juices, producing a succulent, flavorful meal. If you don't have foil, you can fold the salmon packets in parchment paper. If you opt for the parchment, ensure the folded edges are tight and crisp so you don't lose any of the steamy goodness.

10 cups stemmed and shredded stemmed kale
2 scallions, chopped
Sea salt
Freshly ground black pepper
4 (5-ounce) boneless, skinless salmon fillets
2 tablespoons tamari sauce
4 teaspoons apple cider vinegar
2 teaspoons grated peeled fresh ginger
1 teaspoon toasted sesame oil
1 teaspoon minced garlic
Pinch red pepper flakes

Preheat the oven to 400°F.

Lay out 4 (12-by-12-inch) foil squares.

Place 2½ cups of kale and one-fourth of the scallions in the center of each square.

Season lightly with sea salt and pepper.

Place 1 salmon fillet atop each vegetable pile.

In a small bowl, whisk together the tamari sauce, cider vinegar, ginger, sesame oil, garlic, and red pepper flakes.

Spoon equal amounts of the sauce, about 3½ teaspoons, over each fillet.

Fold the foil to form a sealed packet with a little room inside for steam to collect.

Transfer the packets to a baking sheet. Place the sheet in the preheated oven, and bake for about 15 minutes, or until the fish is just cooked through and the kale is tender.

Per Serving Calories: 293; Total Fat: 10g; Sodium: 665mg; Protein: 34g

Braised Chicken with Kale

MEAT LOVERS, SINGLETONS

SERVES 4 / PREP: 20 MINUTES / COOK: 1 HOUR, 20 MINUTES / TOTAL: 1 HOUR, 40 MINUTES

Browning chicken before braising in this kale mixture will ensure an attractive color and pleasing texture to the skin. Cooking in a moist-heat environment doesn't produce any color, just flavor and juicy flesh. If you're watching your fat intake, leave the skin on the chicken while you cook it, and then remove it before eating.

4 chicken thighs, skin on
Sea salt
Freshly ground black pepper
½ cup all-purpose flour
½ teaspoon smoked paprika
2 tablespoons extra-virgin olive oil, divided
2 teaspoons minced garlic
8 cups stemmed and chopped kale
2 cups sodium-free chicken broth
1 tablespoon balsamic vinegar
Pinch red pepper flakes

Preheat the oven to 350°F. Wash the chicken thighs and pat dry with paper towels. Season lightly with sea salt and pepper.

In a small bowl, stir together the flour and paprika. Transfer the mixture to a plate. Dredge the chicken legs in the flour and set them aside. Discard the flour.

In an ovenproof skillet over medium-high heat, heat 1 tablespoon of olive oil. Add the chicken. Brown on both sides, turning once, for about 10 minutes total. Remove the chicken from the pan and set it aside.

To the skillet, add the remaining 1 table-spoon of olive oil and the garlic. Sauté for about 2 minutes, or until softened. Stir in the kale. Sauté for about 6 minutes, tossing with tongs, until wilted and tender.

Add the chicken broth, balsamic vinegar, and red pepper flakes, and stir together. Bring the liquid to a boil. Return the chicken to the skillet, nestling it deeply in the kale mixture.

Cover the skillet with an ovenproof lid, and put it in the oven. Bake for about 1 hour, or until cooked through and tender. Serve the chicken over the braised kale.

Per Serving Calories: 399; Total Fat: 22g; Sodium: 742mg; Protein: 23g

Kale—Vegetable Lasagna

KIDS, LARGE GROUPS, MAKE AHEAD

SERVES 8 / PREP: 40 MINUTES / COOK: 1 HOUR, 5 MINUTES / TOTAL: 1 HOUR, 45 MINUTES

Lasagna is sometimes considered a fattening indulgence, but this recipe is layered with an incredible array of healthy vegetables and tempting herbs. Layer the casserole so it ends with a generous coating of sauce to prevent the noodles from getting too crispy. If you want a gluten-free variation, substitute any gluten-free noodle.

1 tablespoon extra-virgin olive oil
1 red onion, chopped
1 tablespoon minced garlic
1 green zucchini, diced
1 red bell pepper, diced
8 cups stemmed and chopped kale
1 (28-ounce) can sodium-free diced tomatoes
2 tablespoons dried basil
1 tablespoon dried oregano
Pinch red pepper flakes
Sea salt
Freshly ground black pepper
1 (10-ounce) package lasagna noodles, cooked according to package instructions
1 cup shredded mozzarella cheese

Preheat the oven to 400°F. In a large pot over medium-high heat, heat the olive oil.

Add the onion and garlic, and sauté for about 3 minutes, or until softened. Add the zucchini, red bell pepper, and kale. Using tongs, toss for about 6 minutes, or until the kale is wilted and tender.

Stir in the tomatoes, basil, oregano, and red pepper flakes and bring the mixture to a boil. Reduce the heat to low, and simmer for 10 minutes. Remove the sauce from the heat, and season with sea salt and pepper.

In a 9-by-13-inch baking dish, starting and ending with a layer of sauce, make 5 layers of noodles and sauce.

Top the lasagna with the mozzarella cheese, and bake for about 45 minutes, or until bubbly and hot. Cool for 10 to 15 minutes, and serve.

Tip Any gluten-free or regular noodle will work in this casserole, even products labeled "oven ready" that you can layer in dry. If you use a product that needs to be cooked first, keep it soaking in water after it cooks or the noodles will stick together before you can use them in the recipe.

Per Serving Calories: 387; Total Fat: 9g; Sodium: 291mg; Protein: 21g

Chicken & Kale Saffron-Rice Bake

KIDS, MEAT LOVERS, SINGLETONS, ONE POT

SERVES 8 / PREP: 15 MINUTES, PLUS 2 HOURS SOAKING TIME / COOK: 45 MINUTES / TOTAL: 3 HOURS

Saffron is the most expensive spice in the world. It comes from the stigma of crocus flowers, usually from Spain. Each flower has only three stigmas, so it takes almost 5,000 flowers to produce one ounce of saffron threads. Soak saffron a few hours before using it, as steeping allows the color to disperse evenly throughout the food.

6 to 7 saffron threads
2 tablespoons hot water
2 pounds chicken drumsticks
Sea salt
Freshly ground black pepper
4 teaspoons extra-virgin olive oil
1 cup chopped sweet onion
1 teaspoon minced garlic
2 teaspoons lemon zest
Pinch cayenne pepper
2 cups basmati white rice
6 cups stemmed and shredded kale
4 cups low-sodium chicken broth
½ cup slivered almonds

In a small bowl, stir the saffron threads into the hot water. Let stand for 2 hours.

Season the chicken with sea salt and pepper.

In a large, deep skillet over medium-high heat, heat the olive oil.

Add the chicken, and sauté for about 15 minutes, turning, until nicely browned on all sides.

Transfer the chicken to a plate and set aside.

Add the onion and garlic to the skillet, and sauté for about 2 minutes, or until just softened.

Stir in the saffron water, lemon zest, cayenne pepper, and rice. Sauté for about 2 minutes, or until fragrant. Stir in the kale and chicken broth, and bring the mixture to a simmer. Cook for about 4 minutes, or until the kale is just wilted.

Lay the chicken on top of the rice mixture. Cover, and reduce the heat to gently simmer. Cook for about 20 minutes, or until the chicken is cooked completely through and the rice is tender.

Sprinkle with the almonds and serve.

Per Serving Calories: 460; Total Fat: 12g; Sodium: 211mg; Protein: 39g

Simple Maple Salmon with Kale

SERVES 4 / PREP: 15 MINUTES / COOK: 20 MINUTES / TOTAL: 35 MINUTES

Farmed salmon is a good and generally affordable option. If you want wild-caught, try to purchase certified organic or Pacific-caught fish. Salmon has a very high omega-3 fatty acid content, which can cut your risk of heart disease significantly while improving brain and nerve function.

4 (6-ounce) salmon fillets
Sea salt
Freshly ground black pepper
2 tablespoons pure maple syrup, divided
1 tablespoon extra-virgin olive oil
7 cups stemmed and chopped kale
2 tablespoons toasted sesame seeds
1 scallion, thinly sliced on the bias

Preheat the oven to 450°F.

Season the salmon pieces lightly on both sides with sea salt and pepper, and place them in a nonstick baking dish.

Drizzle each fillet with 1½ teaspoons of maple syrup.

Bake the fish for 10 to 12 minutes, or until it flakes easily with a fork.

While the fish is baking, place a large skillet over medium-high heat and add the olive oil.

Add the kale to the skillet. Using tongs, toss for about 6 minutes, or until wilted and tender. Remove from the heat and season with sea salt.

Divide the kale evenly among 4 plates, and top each with a salmon fillet.

Spoon 1½ teaspoons of sesame seeds over each fillet, top with scallions, and serve.

Tip **Maple syrup comes in several grades, ranging from light amber (AA) to a dark grade with a rich caramel taste (B). The darker grade B is the best option for this dish to impart the most flavor to the fish. It's also generally cheaper to purchase.**

Per Serving Calories: 540; Total Fat: 26g; Sodium: 217mg; Protein: 50g

Kale & Shrimp in Wine Sauce

GLUTEN-FREES, SINGLETONS, ONE POT

SERVES 4 / PREP: 20 MINUTES / COOK: 24 MINUTES / TOTAL: 44 MINUTES

Delicate pink shrimp and pale, slender mushrooms served in a brightly accented wine-cream sauce make this dish company-worthy. The sauce alone will inspire your guests to demand chunks of fresh bread for cleaning their plates. Try serving it over angel hair pasta with a dry white wine.

2 tablespoons extra-virgin olive oil, divided
2 pounds (21 to 30 count) shrimp, peeled and deveined
½ sweet onion, thinly sliced
1 tablespoon minced garlic
1 pound oyster mushrooms
2 cups broccoli florets, blanched
1 large carrot, peeled and cut into matchsticks
6 cups stemmed and chopped kale
½ cup dry white wine
¼ cup heavy cream
1 tablespoon chopped fresh basil
Pinch red pepper flakes
Sea salt
Freshly ground black pepper

In a large, deep skillet over medium-high heat, heat 1 tablespoon of olive oil.

Add the shrimp, onion, and garlic, and sauté for about 1 minute, or until the shrimp are pink on one side. Turn the shrimp. Cook for another 1 to 2 minutes, or until the shrimp are pink on both sides. Transfer the shrimp to a plate and set aside.

Return the skillet to the heat, and add the remaining 1 tablespoon of olive oil and the mushrooms, broccoli, and carrots. Sauté for about 8 minutes, or until all the vegetables are tender.

Push the vegetables to the side of the pan. Add the kale to the skillet, tossing with tongs for about 6 minutes, or until the greens are wilted and tender. Add the white wine to the pan and deglaze it, scraping up any browned bits.

Add the shrimp, cream, basil, and red pepper flakes, and cook, stirring, for about 2 minutes, or until the sauce thickens slightly and the shrimp are completely cooked through.

Stir together all the ingredients in the skillet, and season with sea salt and pepper. Serve alone or over pasta.

Per Serving Calories: 522; Total Fat: 13g; Sodium: 721mg; Protein: 61g

Spiced Chicken with Kale & Potato Hash

KIDS, MEAT LOVERS, PALEOS, GLUTEN-FREES, LARGE GROUPS, MAKE AHEAD

SERVES 4 / PREP: 20 MINUTES / COOK: 40 MINUTES / TOTAL: 1 HOUR

Chicken breasts can be prepared in endless ways and show up often on most people's shopping lists and dinner plates. Chicken breasts pair well with almost any vegetable, fruit, herb, or spice, and a four-ounce portion provides almost 70 percent of the recommended daily amount of protein.

¼ teaspoon ground coriander
¼ teaspoon ground cumin
¼ teaspoon ground ginger
⅛ teaspoon ground cinnamon
Pinch sea salt
4 (5-ounce) boneless, skinless chicken breasts
2 tablespoons extra-virgin olive oil, divided
2 pounds cooked potatoes, diced
1 sweet onion, chopped
2 teaspoons minced garlic
Sea salt
Freshly ground black pepper
8 cups stemmed and chopped kale

In a small bowl, stir together the coriander, cumin, ginger, cinnamon, and sea salt. Season the chicken breasts on both sides with the spice mixture.

In a large skillet over medium heat, heat 1 tablespoon of olive oil. Add the chicken, panfrying on both sides until completely cooked through, about 8 minutes per side. Transfer to a plate, and cover with aluminum foil to keep warm.

To the skillet, add the remaining 1 tablespoon of olive oil with the potatoes. Sauté over medium-high heat for about 10 minutes, or until crispy and lightly golden.

Add the onion and garlic, and sauté for about 4 minutes more, or until softened. Season with sea salt and pepper.

Move the potatoes to the side of the skillet, and add the kale. With tongs, toss until wilted and tender, about 6 minutes.

Stir to combine the kale and potatoes in the skillet. Divide the kale and potatoes among 4 plates, top each with 1 piece of chicken, and serve.

Per Serving Calories: 563; Total Fat: 18g; Sodium: 311mg; Protein: 49g

Kale–Turkey Casserole

SERVES 4 / PREP: 15 MINUTES / COOK: 30 MINUTES / TOTAL: 45 MINUTES

Casseroles, which can be made ahead and put in the oven with minimal fuss, help reduce dinner stress at the end of the day. This cheesy, kale-studded casserole can be prepared with chicken instead of turkey, and you can use other grains or seeds like barley or quinoa. For a fancier presentation, top with buttery bread crumbs and sliced fresh tomatoes.

6 cups chopped Blanched Kale (page 33)
4 cups diced turkey meat
4 cups cooked basmati rice
2 tablespoons butter
1 teaspoon minced garlic
2 tablespoons all-purpose flour
2 cups low-sodium chicken broth
1 teaspoon nutmeg
1 cup grated Parmesan cheese
Sea salt
Freshly ground black pepper

Preheat the oven to 350°F.

In a large bowl, mix together the kale, turkey, and rice. Set aside.

In a medium saucepan over medium heat, melt the butter. Add the garlic and sauté for about 2 minutes, or until fragrant.

Whisk in the flour to form a paste. Cook for 1 minute. Continue whisking while adding the chicken broth and nutmeg. Whisk for about 2 minutes, or until the sauce thickens.

Whisk in the Parmesan. Remove the sauce from the heat, and season with sea salt and pepper.

Pour the hot sauce into the kale mixture, and stir until well combined.

Spoon the mixture into a large baking dish, and bake for about 25 minutes, or until warmed through. Serve.

Tip Whenever possible, purchase whole nutmeg kernels and grate your own rather than using a jarred pre-ground product. If you use a lot of nutmeg, invest in a nutmeg grater or mill that easily creates tiny slivers of fresh spice for your dishes.

Per Serving Calories: 590; Total Fat: 16g; Sodium: 494mg; Protein: 39g

Turkey-Kale Chili

SERVES 8 / PREP: 15 MINUTES / COOK: 45 MINUTES / TOTAL: 1 HOUR

Chili is an inexpensive meal that takes little time to prepare; it can even be made ahead and finished in a crockpot. The spiciness of the dish can also be turned up with a couple extra pinches of red pepper flakes. Be forewarned: Do not just keep adding the flakes without giving the flavor a chance to mellow, or you could end up with palate-scorching results.

1 teaspoon extra-virgin olive oil
1 pound extra-lean ground turkey
1 sweet onion, chopped
1 tablespoon minced garlic
1 (15-ounce) can red kidney beans, drained and rinsed
1 (15-ounce) can navy beans, drained and rinsed
1 (15-ounce) can black beans, drained and rinsed
1 (28-ounce) can low-sodium diced tomatoes
3 tablespoons chili powder
2 tablespoons tomato paste
2 tablespoons pure maple syrup
1 teaspoon ground cumin
½ teaspoon red pepper flakes
8 cups stemmed and chopped kale
¼ cup sour cream, divided

In a large stockpot over medium heat, heat the olive oil.

Add the turkey and sauté for 5 minutes, breaking up with a spoon, until cooked through.

With a slotted spoon, move the cooked turkey to the side of the pot. Remove any grease, leaving about 1 teaspoon in the pot.

Combine the onion and garlic with the turkey meat, and sauté for about 3 minutes, or until softened.

Add the kidney beans, navy beans, black beans, diced tomatoes, chili powder, tomato paste, maple syrup, cumin, and red pepper flakes and stir to combine.

Bring to a simmer. Reduce the heat to low, and simmer for about 30 minutes to let the flavors combine. Stir in the kale and simmer for about 6 minutes, stirring frequently, until wilted and tender.

Top each serving with 1 tablespoon of sour cream.

Per Serving Calories: 349; Total Fat: 5g; Sodium: 123mg; Protein: 29g

Sole Kale Florentine

KIDS, GLUTEN-FREES, SINGLETONS, ONE POT

SERVES 4 / PREP: 15 MINUTES / COOK: 20 MINUTES / TOTAL: 35 MINUTES

You can have this gorgeous meal on the table in about 30 minutes, from removing the fish from the refrigerator to putting your napkin in your lap to eat. Fresh fish is always nice because you can see and smell the fillets to ascertain freshness and quality. Sole, however, is one fish you can buy frozen and still get a wonderful product. This fish is often flash frozen a couple hours after being caught, and the texture of the flesh freezes beautifully.

1 tablespoon extra-virgin olive oil
1 sweet onion, chopped
½ teaspoon minced garlic
8 cups stemmed and chopped kale
Sea salt
Freshly ground black pepper
1½ pounds sole fillets
Juice of 1 lemon
1 cup grated Parmesan cheese
Lemon wedges, for serving

Preheat the oven to 350°F.

In a large, ovenproof skillet over medium-high heat, heat the olive oil.

Add the onion and garlic, and sauté for about 3 minutes, or until translucent.

Add the kale to the skillet. Using tongs, toss for about 5 minutes, or until just wilted.

Season with sea salt and pepper.

Remove the skillet from the heat, and spread the kale in the skillet evenly.

Place the fillets atop the kale, squeeze the lemon juice over everything, and top with the Parmesan.

Cover the skillet with an ovenproof lid and put it in the oven. Bake for about 10 minutes, or until the fish flakes easily with a fork and is cooked through. Serve with lemon wedges.

Per Serving Calories: 399; Total Fat: 12g; Sodium: 559mg; Protein: 55g

Sautéed Tomatoes & Kale with Polenta

PALEOS, GLUTEN-FREES, SINGLETONS

SERVES 4 / PREP: 15 MINUTES / COOK: 45 MINUTES / TOTAL: 1 HOUR

This dish's exceptional fragrance will bring to mind rolling green hills and sun-warmed garden herbs as it cooks. Basil produces part of the enticing aroma and has healthy benefits, like being high in disease-busting flavonoids, iron, calcium, and vitamin C. You can swap basil for oregano, thyme, chives, or dill, if you prefer.

4 cups water
1 teaspoon sea salt
1 cup polenta
1 tablespoon extra-virgin olive oil
¼ cup small garlic cloves
Pinch red pepper flakes
1 (28-ounce) can sodium-free diced tomatoes, drained
6 cups stemmed and chopped kale
½ cup shredded fresh basil leaves
½ cup low-sodium chicken broth
Juice of 1 lemon
Sea salt
Freshly ground black pepper

In a large saucepan over medium-high heat, bring the water and salt to a boil and add the polenta, whisking constantly until there are no lumps.

Reduce the heat to low and simmer, whisking frequently, until the polenta starts to thicken, about 5 minutes.

Cover the saucepan and cook, stirring often, until the polenta is creamy and thick and the grains are tender, about 30 minutes.

Remove the polenta from the heat and set aside.

While the polenta is cooking, place a large skillet over medium heat and add the olive oil.

Add the garlic cloves and sauté, stirring frequently, until the garlic is golden and fragrant, about 10 minutes.

Add the red pepper flakes and sauté 1 minute more.

Stir in the tomatoes and sauté for 2 minutes.

⟶

Sautéed Tomatoes & Kale with Polenta, continued

Add the kale, basil, chicken broth, and lemon juice, and cook, stirring, for about 6 minutes, or until the kale is wilted and tender.

Season with sea salt and pepper.

Spoon the polenta into 4 bowls, top with the kale mixture, and serve.

Per Serving Calories: 275; Total Fat: 4g; Sodium: 1,008mg; Protein: 8g

Sausage & Kale Skillet

MEAT LOVERS, GLUTEN-FREES, LARGE GROUPS, ONE POT, MAKE AHEAD

SERVES 4 / PREP: 20 MINUTES / COOK: 55 MINUTES / TOTAL: 1 HOUR, 15 MINUTES

This Mediterranean-influenced stew is spicy, substantial, and attractive with the dark green kale, pale artichoke hearts, and vibrant red bell pepper. You can use any lentil in this dish, but red lentils look gorgeous with the other ingredients. Don't add the artichoke hearts at the beginning of the cooking process, or they will break up.

1 teaspoon extra-virgin olive oil

8 ounces spicy Italian sausage, casings removed

½ sweet onion, sliced

1 tablespoon minced garlic

2 cups low-sodium chicken broth

1 cup dry white wine

1 cup red lentils

1 red bell pepper, thinly sliced

10 cups stemmed and chopped kale

5 artichoke hearts, quartered

Sea salt

Freshly ground black pepper

Pinch red pepper flakes

In a large skillet over medium-high heat, heat the olive oil.

Add the sausage and cook until it is lightly browned, about 6 minutes.

Add the onion and garlic, and sauté for about 3 minutes, or until softened.

Stir in the chicken broth and white wine to deglaze the skillet, scraping up any browned bits. Bring the liquid to a boil.

Stir in the lentils. Reduce the heat to low and simmer for about 35 minutes, or until tender.

Add the red bell pepper and kale.

Cook, stirring, for 6 to 8 minutes, or until the kale is wilted and tender.

Stir in the artichoke hearts, and simmer an additional 2 minutes.

Season with sea salt and pepper, and serve with a pinch of red pepper flakes.

Per Serving Calories: 573; Total Fat: 14g; Sodium: 833mg; Protein: 33g

Kale-Beef Rolls

Cabbage rolls are a traditional dish featuring a ground beef and rice filling stuffed into blanched cabbage leaves and covered in tomato sauce. Kale works just as well as cabbage and provides a little extra nutrition. Don't let the various stages of this recipe scare you away. The preparation is quite simple, and soon you'll be making kale rolls anytime you need a simple meal for a potluck or Sunday dinner.

Sea salt
12 medium kale leaves, stemmed
1 teaspoon salted butter, divided
1 sweet onion, chopped, divided
2 teaspoons minced garlic, divided
1 (15-ounce) can sodium-free
 crushed tomatoes
1 tablespoon ground sweet paprika
2 teaspoons sugar
2 teaspoons apple cider vinegar
Freshly ground black pepper
12 ounces lean ground beef
1½ cups cooked white rice
2 tablespoons chopped fresh oregano
¼ cup beef broth

Preheat the oven to 450°F.

In a large pot of water over high heat, sprinkle sea salt and bring to a boil.

Add the kale leaves and boil for about 8 minutes, or until pliable and soft. Drain and rinse the leaves under cold water, pat them dry, and set aside.

In a medium saucepan over medium-high heat, melt 1 teaspoon of butter.

Add half the onion and 1 teaspoon of garlic, and sauté for about 3 minutes, or until softened.

Stir in the crushed tomatoes, paprika, sugar, and cider vinegar, and bring the mixture to a boil. Reduce the heat to low, and simmer for about 10 minutes, or until the sauce is reduced by one-quarter. Season with sea salt and pepper. Remove from the heat and set aside.

While the sauce is simmering, place a medium skillet over medium-high heat. Add the remaining butter and ground beef and sauté for about 5 minutes, or until cooked through.

Add the remaining onion and 1 teaspoon of garlic to the beef, and sauté for 3 more minutes.

Stir in the cooked rice, oregano, and beef broth, and cook for 2 minutes. Season with sea salt and pepper, and remove from the heat.

Spread about one-fourth of the tomato sauce in a 9-by-9-inch baking dish.

Lay out the kale leaves on a clean work surface. Spoon equal amounts of filling into the center of each. One at a time, tuck in the sides of the leaves and roll tightly. Place the rolls seam-side down in the baking pan.

Cover with the remaining tomato sauce.

Bake for about 15 minutes, or until the sauce is bubbling and the kale rolls are completely heated through, and serve.

Per Serving Calories: 476; Total Fat: 9g; Sodium: 277mg; Protein: 36g

Tomato-Braised Pork Medallions with Kale

MEAT LOVERS, LARGE GROUPS

SERVES 4 / PREP: 20 MINUTES / COOK: 40 MINUTES / TOTAL: 1 HOUR

Pork is consumed more than any other meat worldwide, both fresh and cured as bacon, ham, or sausage. This "white" meat is high in protein, iron, and vitamins B_1, B_2, B_6, and B_{12}. Pork is also low in sodium, and its fat is over 50 percent unsaturated, making pork part of a healthy diet.

4 (4-ounce) boneless pork chops, pounded to a ½-inch thickness
¼ teaspoon sea salt, plus additional for salting the water
Freshly ground black pepper
¼ cup all-purpose flour
10 cups stemmed and chopped kale
2 tablespoons extra-virgin olive oil
2 teaspoons minced garlic
1 cup low-sodium chicken broth
2 tablespoons tomato paste
Cooked rice, for serving

Lightly season the pork chops with sea salt and pepper.

In a shallow dish, dredge the chops in the flour. Set aside.

Place a large pot of water over high heat, add a pinch of sea salt, and bring to a boil. Add the kale and boil for about 10 minutes, or until tender. Drain and set aside. In a large, deep skillet over medium-high heat, heat the olive oil.

Add the garlic and sauté for about 2 minutes, or until fragrant.

Add the pork chops to the skillet, and brown for about 4 minutes, turning once halfway through.

In a small bowl, whisk together the chicken broth and tomato paste.

Add the tomato mixture to the skillet, cover, and simmer the chops for about 15 minutes, or until tender. Add the kale and simmer an additional 5 minutes.

Serve over rice.

Per Serving Calories: 343; Total Fat: 11g; Sodium: 385mg; Protein: 36g

Kale & Beef Stir-Fry

MEAT LOVERS, GLUTEN-FREES, SINGLETONS, ONE POT

SERVES 4 / PREP: 20 MINUTES / COOK: 15 MINUTES / TOTAL: 35 MINUTES

Stir-frying is a quick-cooking technique that utilizes high heat to create delectable dishes featuring perfectly cooked meats and vegetables. The trick to a good stir-fry is to add the ingredients at different times, so each cooks perfectly. This is why the kale is added after the beef—so it stays tender and crisp rather than going limp.

¼ cup natural peanut butter
Juice from 2 oranges
1 tablespoon rice vinegar
1 tablespoon honey
2 teaspoons minced garlic
2 teaspoons tamari sauce
2 teaspoons sesame oil, divided
½ sweet onion, sliced thinly
1 (20-ounce) sirloin steak, trimmed of fat and thinly sliced
8 cups stemmed and chopped kale
¼ cup beef broth
Cooked rice, for serving

In a medium bowl, whisk together the peanut butter, orange juice, rice vinegar, honey, garlic, and tamari sauce until well combined. Set aside.

In a large skillet over medium heat, heat 1 teaspoon of sesame oil.

Add the onion and sauté for about 3 minutes, or until softened.

Add the steak and stir-fry for about 5 minutes, or until cooked to medium and browned.

Transfer the steak and onions to a large bowl and set aside.

Add the remaining 1 teaspoon of sesame oil to the skillet.

Add the kale and beef broth, and sauté for about 6 minutes, or until wilted.

Return the steak, onions, and any accumulated juices.

Stir in the peanut sauce, and cook for 2 minutes, or until heated through.

Serve over rice.

Per Serving Calories: 496; Total Fat: 19g; Sodium: 674mg; Protein: 54g

Special Treat: Chocolate Cake

SERVES 12 / PREP: 30 MINUTES / COOK: 45 MINUTES / TOTAL: 1 HOUR, 40 MINUTES

At this point, you've eaten all the kale you could possibly ever hope to eat—now it's time for some straight-up chocolate cake. This cake is exceptionally moist with the addition of tangy sour cream, and the bittersweet chocolate ensures the flavor is not too sugary. You can also make a dozen large cupcakes instead of a layer cake, but reduce the baking time to 25 minutes.

For the cake

1 cup (2 sticks) unsalted butter, cut into chunks, plus additional for greasing

4 (1-ounce) squares bittersweet chocolate, finely chopped

1½ cups all-purpose flour, plus additional for dusting

¾ cup high-quality cocoa powder

1 tablespoon baking powder

1 teaspoon baking soda

½ teaspoon salt

4 large eggs, beaten

1½ cups granulated sugar

2 teaspoons pure vanilla extract

1 cup sour cream, divided

1 cup mini dark chocolate chips

For the frosting

1 cup (2 sticks) salted butter

¾ cup high-quality cocoa powder

4 ounces high-quality semi-sweet chocolate, melted and cooled

1 teaspoon instant coffee

3 to 3½ cups confectioners' sugar

2 tablespoons heavy cream

To make the cake:

Preheat the oven to 350°F. Grease and flour 2 (8-inch) round cake pans and set aside.

Place a medium saucepan with 2 inches of water in the bottom over medium heat. Set a metal bowl over it, being careful the bowl does not touch the water. Bring the water to a simmer. Reduce the heat to maintain the temperature.

Add the unsalted butter and chopped bittersweet chocolate to the bowl. Stir for 2 to 3 minutes, or until melted and smooth.

Remove the bowl from the heat. Set aside for about 15 minutes, or until the chocolate mixture cools to room temperature.

In a medium bowl, sift together the flour, cocoa powder, baking powder, baking soda, and salt.

→

Chocolate Cake, continued

In a large bowl, using a whisk or hand mixer, beat the eggs, sugar, and vanilla for about 1 minute, or until thoroughly mixed.

Add the cooled chocolate-butter mixture to the eggs, and beat for 1 minute more, or until all ingredients are incorporated.

Add the flour mixture to the chocolate mixture, alternating with the sour cream, in 3 batches, starting and ending with the flour. Mix well after each addition.

Fold the chocolate chips into the batter until evenly distributed.

Spoon the batter into the prepared cake pans and smooth the tops.

Put the cake pans on the middle rack of the preheated oven, and bake for 30 to 35 minutes, or until a toothpick inserted into the center comes out clean and the cake tops spring back when lightly touched.

Remove the cakes from the oven, and cool for 10 minutes.

Run a knife along the edge of the cakes, and carefully pop them out of the pans. Cool completely on wire racks before frosting.

To make the frosting:
In a large bowl, using a hand mixer, beat the butter for about 3 minutes, or until fluffy and pale.

Add the cocoa powder and beat for about 1 minute, or until smooth.

Stir in the melted, cooled chocolate and coffee. Beat for 1 minute to combine.

Add the confectioners' sugar, 1 cup at a time, beating to incorporate after each addition and scraping down the sides of the bowl as needed.

When you achieve the desired sweetness, adjust the thickness of the frosting with the heavy cream as needed.

To assemble the finished cake:
Place 1 cooled cake layer on a cake board or serving plate.

Thickly spread about one-third of the frosting over the layer right to the edge.

Top with the second cooled cake layer, pressing down firmly.

Generously frost the sides of the cake with another one-third of the frosting and the top with the remaining one-third of the frosting.

Cover and refrigerate the cake until ready to serve.

Allow the cake to sit at room temperature for 2 hours to soften the frosting before slicing it into generous pieces.

The Dirty Dozen & Clean Fifteen

A nonprofit and environmental watchdog organization called Environmental Working Group (EWG) looks at data supplied by the U.S. Department of Agriculture (USDA) and the Food and Drug Administration (FDA) about pesticide residues and compiles a list each year of the best and worst pesticide loads found in commercial crops. You can refer to the Dirty Dozen list to know which fruits and vegetables you should always buy organic. The Clean Fifteen list lets you know which produce is considered safe enough when grown conventionally to allow you to skip the organics. This does not mean that the Clean Fifteen produce is pesticide-free, though, so wash these fruits and vegetables thoroughly.

These lists change every year, so make sure you look up the most recent before you fill your shopping cart. You'll find the most recent lists as well as a guide to pesticides in produce at EWG.org/FoodNews.

2015 DIRTY DOZEN

Apples	Peaches
Celery	Potatoes
Cherry tomatoes	Snap peas
Cucumbers	Spinach
Grapes	Strawberries
Nectarines	Sweet bell peppers

In addition to the Dirty Dozen, the EWG added two foods often contaminated with highly toxic organophosphate insecticides:

Hot peppers	Kale/Collard greens

2015 CLEAN FIFTEEN

Asparagus	Mangoes
Avocados	Onions
Cabbage	Papayas
Cantaloupe	Pineapples
Cauliflower	Sweet corn
Eggplant	Sweet peas (frozen)
Grapefruit	Sweet potatoes
Kiwis	

Conversion Tables

VOLUME EQUIVALENTS (LIQUID)

US STANDARD	US STANDARD (OUNCES)	METRIC (APPROXIMATE)
2 tablespoons	1 fl. oz.	30 mL
¼ cup	2 fl. oz.	60 mL
½ cup	4 fl. oz.	120 mL
1 cup	8 fl. oz.	240 mL
1½ cups	12 fl. oz.	355 mL
2 cups or 1 pint	16 fl. oz.	475 mL
4 cups or 1 quart	32 fl. oz.	1 L
1 gallon	128 fl. oz.	4 L

OVEN TEMPERATURES

FAHRENHEIT (F)	CELSIUS (C) (APPROXIMATE)
250°	120°
300°	150°
325°	165°
350°	180°
375°	190°
400°	200°
425°	220°
450°	230°

VOLUME EQUIVALENTS (DRY)

US STANDARD	METRIC (APPROXIMATE)
⅛ teaspoon	0.5 mL
¼ teaspoon	1 mL
½ teaspoon	2 mL
¾ teaspoon	4 mL
1 teaspoon	5 mL
1 tablespoon	15 mL
¼ cup	59 mL
⅓ cup	79 mL
½ cup	118 mL
⅔ cup	156 mL
¾ cup	177 mL
1 cup	235 mL
2 cups or 1 pint	475 mL
3 cups	700 mL
4 cups or 1 quart	1 L

WEIGHT EQUIVALENTS

US STANDARD	METRIC (APPROXIMATE)
½ ounce	15 g
1 ounce	30 g
2 ounces	60 g
4 ounces	115 g
8 ounces	225 g
12 ounces	340 g
16 ounces or 1 pound	455 g

Glossary

AL DENTE: An Italian term meaning "to the tooth", which describes cooking pasta until it is neither too soft nor crunchy, with just a slight resistance when bitten.

AMINO ACIDS: The 20 building blocks of protein.

ANTIOXIDANTS: Includes minerals, vitamins, and phytonutrients crucial for good health as they protect the body from free radicals.

BIAS: To cut on the bias means to cut at a roughly 45-degree angle.

BLOOD GLUCOSE OR BLOOD SUGAR: Level of glucose (sugar) in the blood.

BOLTING: When flowers and seeds are produced suddenly by a plant, usually due to sun exposure and excessive heat.

CALORIES: The amount of energy in food. The higher the number, the more energy the food contains.

CARBOHYDRATES: Organic compounds composed of sugars, starches, and cellulose. The body breaks down carbohydrates into blood sugar, which is used as energy. Carbohydrates can be simple or complex. Complex carbohydrates break down more slowly than simple carbohydrates for more stable blood sugar and include vegetables, fruit, whole grains, and legumes.

CLARIFY: To separate solids from the liquid part of the ingredient, such as butter, and then remove the solids, leaving only the clear liquid portion.

COMPLETE PROTEINS: Proteins that contain all nine essential amino acids. Essential amino acids cannot be produced in the body, so they need to come from foods like dairy, meats, poultry, and seafood.

DEGLAZE: To add liquid to a pan placed over high heat after a food has been sautéed, roasted, or fried in that pan and scrape up all the browned bits left on the bottom, adding flavor to a sauce.

DREDGE: To coat food with flour or another ingredient.

ESSENTIAL AMINO ACIDS: The nine amino acids that the body cannot produce.

ESSENTIAL FATTY ACIDS: Fats not produced in the body that need to be taken from food, as they are crucial for proper physical functioning. The most well-known essential fatty acids are omega-3 and omega-6.

FIBER: The indigestible component in plants that sweeps through the body like a broom. It is crucial for a healthy, efficient digestive system. A diet high in fiber can help prevent some types of cancer, diabetes, heart disease, and other health problems.

FLAVONOIDS: Natural pigments found in plants that function as antioxidants to help protect human cells from damage.

FREE RADICALS: Oxygen or nitrogen molecules that are missing electrons, so they try to take electrons from cells in the body, causing damage. Unchecked, free radicals can damage cells in many ways.

GLUTEN: A cereal grain protein that can cause health problems in people with gluten sensitivity.

GLYCEMIC INDEX: The measure of how fast a food causes blood sugar to rise after consuming it.

HARDY: Describes a plant that does not need protection to withstand frost exposure.

HEIRLOOM: A plant that has been unchanged for between 50 to 100 years through open-pollenated hybridization.

INSULIN: Hormone that moves glucose from the blood into the body's cells.

JULIENNE: To cut ingredients into thin strips.

MACRONUTRIENTS: Main groups of nutrients your body uses for essential tasks. They include protein, carbohydrates, and fat.

OMEGA-3 FATTY ACID: A family of three fats (ALA, EPA, and DHA) not produced in the body but essential for health. Omega-3s help with almost every type of cell activity.

OMEGA-6 FATTY ACID: Unsaturated fatty acids not made by the body but crucial for good health.

PHYTONUTRIENTS: Beneficial compounds found only in plants that may help prevent disease and keep your body functioning smoothly.

PROTEIN: Essential nutrient made from amino acids that is used for many body functions as well as maintaining and building cells.

References

Ambrosone, Christine B., Li Tang. "Cruciferous Vegetable Intake and Cancer Prevention: Role of Nutrigenetics." *Cancer Prevention Research* 2, no. 4 (April 2009): 298–300. doi:10.1158/1940-6207. CAPR-09-0037.

Butler, Carolyn. "Eat Your Kale." *The Washington Post.* September 24, 2012. Accessed January 5, 2015. http://washingtonpost.com/national/health-science/eat-your-kale/2012/09/24/95a4d756-018f-11e2-9367-4e1bafb958db_story.html.

Chu, Michael, and Terry F. Seltzer. "Myxedema Coma Induced by Ingestion of Raw Bok Choy." *New England Journal of Medicine* 2010, no. 362 (May 2010): 1945–46. doi:10.1056/NEJMc0911005.

Clarke, John D., Roderick H. Dashwood, and Emily Ho. "Multi-Targeted Prevention of Cancer by Sulforaphane." *Cancer Letters* 269, no. 2 (October 2008): 291–304. doi:10.1016/j.canlet.2008.04.018.

Davidson, Alan. *The Oxford Companion to Food.* Oxford: Oxford University Press, 1999.

Environmental Working Group. "EWG's 2014 Shopper's Guide to Pesticides in Produce." Accessed January 6, 2015. www.ewg.org/foodnews/summary.php.

Fuhrman, Joel. *The End of Dieting: How to Live for Life.* New York: HarperOne, 2014.

Giovannucci, E., E. B. Rimm, Y. Liu, M. J. Stampfer, and W. C. Willett. "A Prospective Study of Cruciferous Vegetables and Prostate Cancer." *Cancer Epidemiology, Biomarkers & Prevention* 12, no. 12 (December 2003): 1403–9. doi:10.1038/sj.pcan.4500979.

Greene, Bert. *Greene on Greens & Grains.* New York: Tess Press, 2000.

Harvard School of Public Health. "Fiber: Start Roughing It!" The Nutrition Source. Accessed January 5, 2015. www.hsph.harvard.edu/nutritionsource/what-should-you-eat/fiber-full-story/.

Hecht, S. S. "Inhibition of Carcinogenesis by Isothiocyanates." *Drug Metabolism Reviews* 32, nos. 3–4 (August–November 2003): 395–411. doi:10.1081/DMR-100102342.

Higdon, Jane V., Barbara Delage, David E. Williams, and Roderick H. Dashwood. "Cruciferous Vegetables and Human Cancer Risk: Epidemiologic Evidence and Mechanistic Basis." *Pharmacological Research* 55, no. 3 (March 2007): 224–36. doi:10.1016/j.phrs.2007.01.009.

Kahlon, T. S., M. C. Chiu, and M. H. Chapman. "Steam Cooking Significantly Improves In Vitro Bile Acid Binding of Collard Greens, Kale, Mustard Greens, Broccoli, Green Bell Pepper, and Cabbage." *Nutrition Research* 28, no. 6 (June 2008): 351–57. doi:10.1016/j.nutres.2008.03.007.

Kiple, Kenneth F., and Kriemhild Coneè Ornelas, eds. *The Cambridge World History of Food*. Cambridge: Cambridge University Press, 2000.

Margen, Sheldon, and the Editors of the University of California at Berkeley Wellness Letter. *The Wellness Encyclopedia of Food and Nutrition: How to Buy, Store, and Prepare Every Variety of Fresh Food*. New York: Rebus, 1992.

Miller, Jessica A., Kirk Pappan, Patricia A. Thompson, Elizabeth J. Want, Alexandros P. Siskos, Hector C. Keun, Jacob Wulff, Chengcheng Hu, Julie E. Lang, and H. H. Sherry Chow. "Plasma Metabolomic Profiles of Breast Cancer Patients after Short-Term Limonene Intervention." *Cancer Prevention Research* 8, no. 1 (January 2015): doi:10.1158/1940-6207. CAPR-14-0100.

Mindell, Earl. *Earl Mindell's Food as Medicine: What You Can Eat to Help Prevent Everything from Colds to Heart Disease to Cancer*. New York: Fireside, 1994.

National Cancer Institute. "Cruciferous Vegetables and Cancer Prevention." Accessed January 5, 2015. www.cancer .gov/cancertopics/factsheet/diet /cruciferous-vegetables.

Roberts, Jonathan. *The Origins of Fruits and Vegetables*. New York: Universe, 2001.

Robinson, Jo. *Eating on the Wild Side: The Missing Link to Optimum Health*. New York: Little Brown, 2013.

Root, Waverley. *Food: An Authoritative and Visual History and Dictionary of the Foods of the World*. New York: Smithmark, 1996.

Tang, Li, Gary R. Zirpoli, K. Guru, K. B. Moysich, Y. Zhang, C. B. Ambrosone, and S. E. McCann. "Consumption of Raw Cruciferous Vegetables Is Inversely Associated with Bladder Cancer Risk." *Cancer Epidemiology Biomarkers & Prevention* 4 (April 2008): 938–44. doi:10.1158/1055-9965.EPI-07-2502.

USDA National Nutrient Database for Standard Reference Release 27. "Basic Report: 11233, Kale, Raw." Accessed January 5, 2015. http://ndb.nal.usda.gov /ndb/foods/show/3018.

USDA National Nutrient Database for Standard Reference Release 27. "Basic Report: 11234, Kale, Cooked, Boiled, Drained, without Salt." Accessed January 5, 2015. http://ndb.nal.usda.gov/ndb/foods /show/3019.

WebMD. "The Truth About Kale." Food & Recipes Center, WebMD. Accessed January 5, 2015. www.webmd.com/food-recipes /features/the-truth-about-kale.

Whole Foods Market. "ANDI Guide." Accessed January 5, 2015. http:// wholefoodsmarket.com/healthy-eating /health-starts-here/resources-and-tools /top-ten-andi-scores.

Wood, Rebecca. *The New Whole Foods Encyclopedia: A Comprehensive Resource for Healthy Eating*. New York: Penguin Books, 1999.

Resources

WEBSITES

Discover Kale
www.discoverkale.co.uk

Self-Nutrition Data—Kale
http://nutritiondata.self.com/facts
/vegetables-and-vegetable-products/2461/2

The Old Farmer's Almanac
www.almanac.com/plant/kale

Web MD—The Truth about Kale
www.webmd.com/food-recipes/kale
-nutrition-and-cooking

World's Healthiest Foods—Kale
www.whfoods.com

RESOURCES

Kale Seeds

Burpee
www.burpee.com

Hawthorn Farm Organic Seeds
http://hawthornfarm.ca

High Mowing Organic Seeds
www.highmowingseeds.com

Incredible Seeds
http://incredibleseeds.ca

Johnny Seeds
www.johnnyseeds.com

Seed Savers Exchange
www.seedsavers.org

Veseys
http://veseys.com

West Coast Seeds
http://westcoastseeds.com

Growing Kale

Canadian Gardening
http://canadiangardening.com

Gardening About.com
http://gardening.about.com

Gardening Cornell University
http://gardening.cornell.edu

Heirloom Organics
http://heirloom-organics.com

USA Gardener
http://usagardener.com

Index

Photo Credits